LEADING A JOY-FILLED LIFE

Jesus Calling® Bible Study Series

Volume 1: Experiencing God's Presence

Volume 2: Trusting in Christ

Volume 3: Receiving Christ's Hope

Volume 4: Living a Life of Worship

Volume 5: Giving Thanks to God

Volume 6: Living with God's Courage

Volume 7: Dwelling in God's Peace

Volume 8: Putting Jesus First

Jesus Always Bible Study Series

Volume 1: Embracing Jesus' Love

Volume 2: Following God's Direction

Volume 3: Leading a Joy-Filled Life

Volume 4: Walking in God's Grace

JESUS ALWAYS BIBLE STUDY SERIES

LEADING A JOY-FILLED LIFE

EIGHT SESSIONS

with Karen Lee-Thorp

THOMAS NELSON
Since 1798

Published in Nashville, Tennessee, by Thomas Nelson. Thomas Nelson is a registered trademark of HarperCollins Christian Publishing, Inc.

All Scripture quotations, unless otherwise noted, are taken from The Holy Bible, New International Version®, niv®. Copyright © 1973, 1978, 1984, 2011 by Biblica, Inc.® Used by permission. All rights reserved worldwide.

Scripture quotations marked kjv are taken from the King James Version. Public domain.

ISBN 978-0-310-09136-3

First Printing January 2018 / Printed in the United States of America

CONTENTS

Introduction   vii

SESSION 1 JOY IN SALVATION   1
   1 Peter 1:3–9

SESSION 2 JOY IN RESTORATION   13
   Luke 24:36–53

SESSION 3 JOY THAT TRANSCENDS CIRCUMSTANCES   25
   Habakkuk 3:16–19

SESSION 4 JOY AND STRENGTH   37
   Nehemiah 8:5–12

SESSION 5 JOY DESPITE FEAR   49
   Matthew 28:1–10

SESSION 6 JOY AND HEALING   61
   Psalm 30:1–12

SESSION 7 JOY IN SINGING   73
   1 Chronicles 16:23–33

SESSION 8 JOY EVEN IN SUFFERING   85
   Acts 16:16–34

Leader's Notes   99

INTRODUCTION

Sometimes our busy and difficult lives give us the impression that God is silent. We cry out to Him, but our feelings tell us He isn't answering our prayers. In this, our feelings are incorrect. God hears the prayers of His children and speaks directly into the situations in which we find ourselves. The trouble is that our lives are often too hectic, our minds too distracted, for us to take in what He offers.

This *Jesus Always* Bible study is designed to help individuals and groups meditate on the words of Scripture and hear them not just as words said to people long ago but as words said to us today in the here and now. The goal is to help the heart open up and respond to what the mind reads—to encounter the living God as He speaks through the Scriptures. The writer to the Hebrews tells us:

In the past God spoke to our ancestors through the prophets at many times and in various ways, but in these last days he has spoken to us by his Son, whom he appointed heir of all things, and through whom also he made the universe. The Son is the radiance of God's glory and the exact representation of his being, sustaining all things by his powerful word.

—HEBREWS 1:1–3

God has spoken to us through His Son, Jesus Christ. The New Testament gives us the chance to walk with Jesus, see what He does, and hear Him speak into the sometimes-confusing situations in which we find ourselves. The Old Testament tells the story of how God prepared a people to be the family of Jesus, and in the experiences of those men and women, we find our own lives mirrored.

THE GOAL OF THIS SERIES

The *Jesus Always Bible Study Series* offers you a chance to lay down your cares, enter God's Presence, and hear Him speak through His Word. You will get to spend some time silently studying a passage of Scripture, and then, if you're meeting with a group, openly sharing your insights and hearing what others discovered. You'll also get to discuss excerpts from the *Jesus Always* devotional that relate to the themes of the Bible passages. In this way, you will learn how to better make space in your life for the Spirit of God to speak to you through the Word of God and the people of God.

THE FLOW OF EACH SESSION

Each session of this study guide contains the following elements:

- CONSIDER IT. The two questions in this opening section serve as an icebreaker to help you start thinking about the theme of the session, connecting it to your own past or present experience, and allowing you to get to know the others in your group more deeply. If you've had a busy day and your mind is full of distractions, these questions can help you better focus.

- EXPERIENCE IT. Here you will find two readings from *Jesus Always* along with some questions for reflection. This is your chance to talk with others about the biblical principles found within the *Jesus Always* devotions. Can you relate to what each reading describes? What insights from God's Word does it illuminate? What does it motivate you to do? This section will assist you in applying these biblical principles to your everyday habits.

- STUDY IT. Next you'll explore a Scripture passage connected to the session topic and the readings from *Jesus Always*. You will not only analyze these Bible passages but also pray through them in ways designed to engage your heart and your head. You'll first talk with your group about what the verse or verses mean and then spend several minutes in silence, letting God speak into your life through His Word.

- LIVE IT. Finally, you will find five days' worth of suggested Scripture passages that you can pray through on your own during the week. Suggested questions for additional study and reflection are provided.

FOR LEADERS

If you are leading a group through this study guide, please see the Leader's Notes at the end of the guide. You'll find background on the design of the study as well as suggested answers for some of the study questions.

JOY IN SALVATION

CONSIDER IT

Billy Bray was a twenty-nine-year-old miner in Cornwall, England, when he had a brush with death on the job in 1823. He was known as a rowdy drinker and womanizer, but shortly after the mining accident, he read John Bunyan's *Visions of Heaven and Hell* and was convicted that he was on his way to hell. He became a passionate Christian and unconventional preacher, often bursting into singing, shouting for joy, and dancing in the middle of a sermon. Many hearers complained about this behavior, but Bray was so grateful for God's rescue from the path of destruction that he couldn't—and *wouldn't*—stop celebrating.

If you are a follower of Christ, what feelings and emotions does that evoke in you? Does your liberation from the enemy fill you with such joy that you can't help but let everybody you meet know about it? Perhaps you're not the type who sings and dances. Perhaps for you, joy is a deep and settled sense of peace, a sense that you're okay and nothing can take away your well-being. Yet regardless of how you experience joy, it's important to recognize the amazing gift that God has given to His children—and be incredibly thankful for it.

In this session, we'll examine what the disciple Peter has to say about the inexpressible and glorious joy we should all have when we think about what God has done for us. We will see that no amount of persecution could shake Peter's joy once he had seen Jesus risen from the dead and heard His promises about our future life.

1. *When you were a child, what was something that filled you with joy?*

2. *When you were a child, what was something that could rob you of joy?*

_____

_____

EXPERIENCE IT

In Me you can discover *Joy inexpressible and full of Glory*! You will not find this kind of pleasure anywhere else; it is available only in your relationship with Me. So trust Me, beloved, and walk confidently along your life-path. As we journey together, you will encounter many obstacles—some of which are quite painful. Expect these difficulties each day, and don't let them throw you off course. Refuse to let adversity keep you from enjoying Me. In My Presence deep sorrow can coexist with even deeper Joy.

Your life with Me is an adventure, and there are always some dangers involved in adventurous journeys. Ask Me to give you courage so that you can face your troubles boldly. Keep your hope fully fastened on Me and on the heavenly reward that awaits you. Your Joy will expand astronomically—beyond anything you could possibly imagine—when you reach your eternal home. There you will see Me *face to Face*, and your Joy will know no bounds!

—FROM *JESUS ALWAYS*, JANUARY 8

3. *As a follower of Christ, how can you refuse to let adversity keep you from enjoying God? What chosen actions does that refusal involve?*

_____

_____

_____

4. *In 1 Corinthians 2:9, Paul writes, "No eye has seen . . . no ear has heard, and . . . no human mind has conceived—the things God has prepared for those who love him." How do you picture heaven and the eternal life that God has in store for His children?*

I offer you *inexpressible and glorious Joy*—straight from heaven itself! This *triumphant, heavenly Joy* can be found only in Me. It is easy to slide, ever so gradually, from delighting in Me to living for the next spiritual "high." Sometimes I bless you with a taste of heaven's splendor, but the primary purpose of these experiences is to whet your appetite for the next life. Do not underestimate the brokenness of the world you inhabit. Your enjoyment of My Presence will always intermingle with the sorrows of living in this fallen world—until *I take you into Glory.*

Someday you will see Me face to Face, but for now *you love Me without having seen Me. You believe in Me even though you do not see Me.* This love for Me is not irrational or whimsical. It's a response to My boundless passion for you, dramatically displayed on the cross and verified by My resurrection. You worship a risen, living Savior! *Blessed are those who have not seen Me and yet have believed.*

—FROM *JESUS ALWAYS*, FEBRUARY 12

5. *How is the joy that followers of Christ experience different than a mere emotion?*

6. *How does the cross give followers of Christ a reason for joy?*

STUDY IT

Read 1 Peter 1:3–9. In this passage, Peter lays the foundation for his letter by praising God for his salvation. Peter's words point to the present aspect of salvation—the new birth—but there is also a much-longed-for future salvation that is yet to be revealed. Note that *mercy* can be defined as the compassion God shows to human beings despite their sin and because of their helplessness to right their own wrongs. The *inheritance* to which Peter refers is eternal life in God's joyous kingdom, where the deepest longings of every believer's heart will be fulfilled.

> [3] Praise be to the God and Father of our Lord Jesus Christ! In his great mercy he has given us new birth into a living hope through the resurrection of Jesus Christ from the dead, [4] and into an inheritance that can never perish, spoil or fade. This inheritance is kept in heaven for you, [5] who through faith are shielded by God's power until the coming of the salvation that is ready to be revealed in the last time. [6] In all this you greatly rejoice, though now for a little while you may have had to suffer grief in all kinds of trials. [7] These have come so that the proven genuineness of your faith—of greater worth than gold, which perishes even though refined by fire—may result in praise, glory and honor when Jesus Christ is revealed. [8] Though you have not seen him, you love him; and even though you do not see him now, you believe in him and are filled with an inexpressible and glorious joy, [9] for you are receiving the end result of your faith, the salvation of your souls.

7. *How does the resurrection of Jesus give His followers a living hope (see verse 3)? What are they hoping for?*

_____

_____

_____

_____

8. *If you are a Christ-follower, what gives you joy when you think about the inheritance you have in store for you?*

_____

_____

_____

_____

9. *What role does faith have in securing the inheritance promised to Christians (see verse 5)?*

_____

_____

_____

_____

10. *According to verse 7, what role do trials have in the life of faith?*

_____

_____

_____

11. *Are you filled with an inexpressible and glorious joy because of your love for Jesus (verse 8)? If so, what fosters that joy in you? What can get in the way?*

12. *Take two minutes of silence to reread the passage, looking for a sentence, phrase, or even one word that stands out as something Jesus may want you to focus on in your life. If you're meeting with a group, the leader will keep track of time. At the end of two minutes, you may share with the group the word or phrase that came to you in the silence.*

13. *Read the passage aloud again. Take another two minutes of silence, prayerfully considering what response God might want you to make to what you have read in His Word. If you're meeting with a group, the leader will again keep track of time. At the end of two minutes, you may share with the group what came to you in the silence if you wish.*

14. *If you're meeting with a group, how can the members pray for you? If you're using this study on your own, what would you like to say to God right now?*

_____

_____

_____

LIVE IT

At the end of each session you'll find suggested Scripture readings for spending time alone with God during five days of the coming week. This week, each reading will focus on the joy of salvation (both physical and spiritual) as portrayed in the book of Psalms. Read each passage slowly, pausing to think about what is being said. Rather than approaching this as an assignment to complete, think of it as an opportunity to meet with the One who loves you most. Use any of the questions that are helpful.

Day 1

Read Psalm 27:4–6. What gives the psalmist joy in this passage?

_____

_____

_____

What is the modern equivalent of seeking the Lord in His temple?

_____

_____

_____

Have you experienced the Lord keeping you safe in His dwelling? If so, how?

_____

_____

_____

Today, consider setting aside a special place where you will go each day to meet with the Lord.

Day 2

Read Psalm 28:6–9. What causes the psalmist to praise God in this passage?

_____

_____

_____

How have you experienced the Lord hearing your cry for mercy?

_____

_____

_____

What joy does it give you to picture the Lord as the fortress for His children?

_____

_____

_____

Ask God to be your strength and fortress today—and watch for how He answers that prayer.

Day 3

Read Psalm 33:1–5. What reasons for being joyful does this psalmist provide (see verses 4–5)?

How have you seen the truth of these two verses in your own life?

Are you the kind of person who "shouts" for joy? Why do you suppose that's the case?

Rejoice today that the word of the Lord is right and true.

Day 4

Read Psalm 42:1–4. Can you identify with this psalmist thirsting for God? What does that look like in your life?

Who or what are the voices in your life that whisper, "Where is your God?" (verse 3)

_____

_____

_____

What does this psalmist do to help him remember God's salvation and deliverance (see verse 4)?

_____

_____

_____

Pour out your soul to God today, and see if that leads to deeper joy.

Day 5

Read Psalm 43:1–4. What was the general life circumstance in which this psalmist found himself?

_____

_____

_____

How could he nevertheless be joyful that God was his salvation?

_____

_____

_____

What do you think the psalmist means when he asks God to "send me your light" (verse 3)? What is the light that God sends to His children?

_____

_____

_____

Express your joy to God today for offering you His gift of salvation.

JOY IN RESTORATION

CONSIDER IT

General André Masséna was a French general who served under Napoleon in the late eighteenth century. At one point, Masséna led an army of 18,000 men against a defenseless Austrian town. The town leaders were going to surrender, but because it was Easter, they decided to hold church services first.

All the church bells in that place rang out for joy that day, in spite of the threat that was headed their way. Remarkably, when the services were over, the townspeople found that the French army had retreated. Apparently, when the French heard the celebratory bells, they concluded that an Austrian army had arrived to defend the town. Masséna wasn't prepared to engage with such a force, so he retreated.

Easter, the joyful celebration of Jesus' resurrection, is the day of days in the history of the world. It is the day on which God reconciled "the world to himself in Christ, not counting people's sins against them" (2 Corinthians 5:19). It is as if we were the Austrian villagers surrounded by the French enemy, with no hope in sight, but then the bells rang out and the enemy fled. We can now choose to experience the joy that comes from deliverance in Christ and being restored in fellowship with God.

In this session, we will look at the empty tomb and seek to understand how God used this event to reconcile Himself with each of us. As we join the disciples in their joy at Christ's resurrection, we will seek to let this amazing truth ring out inside us too.

1. *Did you celebrate Easter when you were a child? If so, what did you do?*

2. *What does Easter mean to you today?*

_____

_____

_____

EXPERIENCE IT

I am the Risen One—your *living God.* Celebrate the Joy of serving a Savior who is exuberantly alive! Rejoice also in My promise to be with you continually—throughout time and eternity. These truths can sustain you through the greatest trials or disappointments you will ever encounter. So walk boldly along the path of Life with Me, trusting confidently in the One who never lets go of your hand.

Consider what I offer you: Myself, forgiveness of *all* your sins, forever-pleasures in heaven. This is all so extravagant and lavish that you cannot comprehend it fully. That is why worshiping Me is so important: It's a powerful way of connecting with Me that transcends your understanding. It also proclaims My Presence. There are numerous ways of worshiping Me: singing hymns and praise songs, studying and memorizing My Word, praying individually and with others, glorying in the wonders of My creation. Serving and loving others with My Love can also be worship. *Whatever you do, do it all for the Glory of God—My Glory!*

—FROM *JESUS ALWAYS,* MARCH 23

3. *When you think of Jesus as the Risen Lord, what thoughts, images, and feelings does that evoke within you?*

_____

_____

_____

4. *Do you experience joy when you think about Jesus' offer to be with you now and forever? Why did you answer the way you did?*

_____

_____

_____

I am your Joy! These four words can light up your life. Since I am always with you, *the Joy of My Presence* is continually accessible to you. You can open up to My Presence through your trust in Me, your love for Me. Try saying, "Jesus, You are my Joy." My Light will shine upon you and within you as you *rejoice in Me*, your Savior. Ponder all I have done for you and all that I am to you. This will lift you up above your circumstances.

When you became My follower, I empowered you to rise above the conditions in your life. I filled you with My Spirit, and this Holy Helper has limitless Power. I promised that *I will come back and take you to be with Me* in heaven—*that you may be where I am* forever. Whenever your world is looking dark, brighten your perspective by focusing on Me. Relax in My Presence, and hear Me saying, "Beloved, I am your Joy!"

—From *Jesus Always*, January 2

5. *How does it affect you to say, "Jesus, you are my joy"?*

_____

_____

_____

6. *If you are a Christ-follower, what helps you focus on Jesus? What gets in the way?*

_____

_____

_____

STUDY IT

Read Luke 24:36–53. This scene takes place on the evening of the Sunday when Jesus rose from the dead—God's ultimate act of restoration with sinful humankind. By this point, Jesus has already appeared to some of the women among His followers and to two disciples on a road. The apostles are talking about this when suddenly Jesus is there among them in the locked room where they have been hiding. They believe that all righteous people will be raised from the dead at the end of time, but they don't believe one man can be raised while the rest of life goes on as normal. They have seen Lazarus raised (see John 11), but still they don't believe their eyes in this moment.

[36] While they were still talking about this, Jesus himself stood among them and said to them, "Peace be with you."

[37] They were startled and frightened, thinking they saw a ghost. [38] He said to them, "Why are you troubled, and why do doubts rise in your minds? [39] Look at my hands and my feet. It is I myself! Touch me and see; a ghost does not have flesh and bones, as you see I have."

[40] When he had said this, he showed them his hands and feet. [41] And while they still did not believe it because of joy and amazement, he asked them, "Do you have anything here to eat?" [42] They gave him a piece of broiled fish, [43] and he took it and ate it in their presence.

[44] He said to them, "This is what I told you while I was still with you: Everything must be fulfilled that is written about me in the Law of Moses, the Prophets and the Psalms."

[45] Then he opened their minds so they could understand the Scriptures. [46] He told them, "This is what is written: The Messiah will suffer and rise from the dead on the third day, [47] and repentance for the forgiveness of sins will be preached in his name to all nations, beginning at Jerusalem. [48] You are witnesses of these things. [49] I am going to send you what my Father has promised; but stay in the city until you have been clothed with power from on high."

⁵⁰ When he had led them out to the vicinity of Bethany, he lifted up his hands and blessed them. ⁵¹ While he was blessing them, he left them and was taken up into heaven. ⁵² Then they worshiped him and returned to Jerusalem with great joy. ⁵³ And they stayed continually at the temple, praising God.

7. *What does Jesus do to convince His followers that He really is alive in a body?*

8. *Why does it matter that Jesus was raised with a body and is not just "spiritually" alive?*

9. *How do the disciples' emotions change over the course of this passage?*

10. *What are your feelings toward Jesus' resurrection? Does it seem distant from you because you haven't seen Jesus alive in the flesh for yourself? Describe your response to this story.*

11. *Why is the story of Christ's resurrection such a central focus of joy for Christians?*

12. *Take two minutes of silence to reread the passage, looking for a sentence, phrase, or even one word that stands out as something Jesus may want you to focus on in your life. If you're meeting with a group, the leader will keep track of time. At the end of two minutes, you may share with the group the word or phrase that came to you in the silence.*

13. *Read the passage aloud again. Take another two minutes of silence, prayerfully considering what response God might want you to make to what you have read in His Word. If you're meeting with a group, the leader will again keep track of time. At the end of two minutes, you may share with the group what came to you in the silence if you wish.*

14. *If you're meeting with a group, how can the members pray for you? If you're using this study on your own, what would you like to say to God right now?*

LIVE IT

This week, each reading will celebrate the joy of being restored to God as portrayed in Psalm 51. Read each passage slowly, pausing to think about what is being said. Rather than approaching this as an assignment to complete, think of it as an opportunity to meet with the One who loves you most. Use any of the questions that are helpful.

Day 1

Read Psalm 51:1–4. This is a psalm that David wrote after the prophet Nathan confronted him for committing the sin of adultery with Bathsheba (see 2 Samuel 11–12). How would you describe David's emotional state as he wrote this psalm?

What does David request of the Lord (see verses 1–2)? What is he seeking?

What does David say is true about the Lord (see verse 4)?

_____

_____

_____

Today, take a few minutes to rejoice in God's offer of mercy and unfailing love.

Day 2

Read Psalm 51:5–6. What does David acknowledge about himself?

_____

_____

_____

What does he acknowledge that God desires from him?

_____

_____

_____

How does David say that God has helped him to do this? For how long has God helped him?

_____

_____

_____

Thank God that He offers His wisdom and guidance to you when you ask.

Day 3

Read Psalm 51:7–12. Why does sin sap our joy? Why does forgiveness help to restore it?

_____

_____

_____

What do you think David means when he writes, "let the bones you have crushed rejoice" (verse 8)?

_____

_____

_____

What does David want to have restored (see verse 12)?

_____

_____

_____

Today, be honest with God about your sin, and rejoice that He willingly offers to forgive you.

Day 4

Read Psalm 51:13–15. What does David say he will do when he experiences the restoration he is seeking with God (see verse 13)?

_____

_____

_____

If you've ever experienced restoration with God, how has it led you to "sing" of His righteousness (see verse 14)?

_____

_____

_____

_____

_____

What prayer of thanksgiving and rejoicing do you need to say to God today?

_____

_____

_____

_____

Let your mouth declare God's praises to those in your world as you go through your day.

Day 5

Read Psalm 51:16–19. What does David mean when he says that God does not "delight in sacrifice" (verse 16)?

_____

_____

_____

_____

What does David say is his "sacrifice" that is pleasing to the Lord (see verse 17)?

_____

_____

_____

_____

What is something in your life today that you would like to see restored for God's glory?

_____

_____

_____

_____

Take joy in knowing that God wants to be restored to you, and thank Him for it today.

JOY THAT
TRANSCENDS
CIRCUMSTANCES

CONSIDER IT

Viktor Frankl was an Austrian psychiatrist who endured the Nazi death camps in World War II. After his release, he pondered why some people survived the horrible conditions while others succumbed. He wrote about this in his book *Man's Search for Meaning*. Author Stephen Covey summarizes Frankl's conclusions:

> He looked at several factors—health, vitality, family structure, intelligence, survival skills. Finally he concluded that none of these factors was primarily responsible. The single most significant factor, he realized, was a sense of future vision—the impelling conviction of those who were to survive that they had a mission to perform, some important work left to do.[1]

Faith in Jesus offers this kind of strong, future-oriented vision. Faith can see those who believe in Him through the worst of circumstances, reminding them they have things to do in this life and a wondrous future beyond death. In this session, we'll learn that joy can prevail even in dire situations—when we focus on God's presence and God's promises.

1. *When you consider your future, what are you looking forward to? What are you dreading?*

2. *Do you have a sense of purpose about your life? If so, what do you believe you're meant to do with it? If not, how does that affect you?*

EXPERIENCE IT

The Joy I give you transcends your circumstances. This means that no matter what is happening in your life, it is possible to be joyful in Me. The prophet Habakkuk listed a series of dire circumstances that he was anticipating, then he proclaimed: *"Yet I will rejoice in the Lord, I will be joyful in God my Savior."* This is transcendent Joy!

I am training you to view your life from a heavenly perspective—through eyes of faith. When things don't go as you had hoped, talk with Me. *Seek My Face* and My guidance. I will help you discern whether you need to work to change the situation or simply accept it. Either way, you can teach yourself to say: "I can still rejoice in *You*, Jesus." This short statement of faith—expressing your confidence in Me—will change your perspective dramatically. As you practice doing this more and more, your Joy will increase. This training also prepares you to handle the difficulties awaiting you on your pathway toward heaven. *Rejoice in Me always.*

—From *Jesus Always*, February 5

3. *What circumstances in your life make it challenging for you to live with joy?*

_____

_____

_____

4. *What would it look like for you to view your circumstances from a heavenly perspective—through eyes of faith? What difference could this make in your life?*

_____

_____

_____

Find Joy in Me, for I am your Strength. It is vital to keep your Joy alive, especially when you're in the throes of adversity. Whenever you are struggling with difficulties, you need to guard your thoughts and spoken words carefully. If you focus too much on all the things that are wrong, you will become increasingly discouraged—and your strength will be sapped. As soon as you realize what is happening, stop this hurtful process immediately. Turn to Me, asking Me to help you with all your struggles.

Take time to praise Me: Speak or sing words of worship. Read scriptures that help you rejoice in Me.

Remember that your problems are temporary but *I* am eternal— and so is your relationship with Me. As you find Joy in Me, delighting in *My unfailing Love* for you, your strength will increase. This is *the Joy of the Lord,* which is yours for all time and throughout eternity!

—From *Jesus Always,* January 4

5. *Why is it important for you to guard your thoughts and words carefully (see Proverbs 4:23)?*

_____

_____

_____

_____

6. *What should you do if you notice that you are being dragged down by circumstances?*

_____

_____

_____

_____

STUDY IT

Read Habakkuk 3:16–19. Habakkuk was a prophet in Jerusalem shortly before 600 BC. He saw the corruption in Israel and asked God what He was going to do about it. God replied that He was sending the Babylonians to destroy the nation. Habakkuk was appalled, but he ultimately came to grips with the fact that this was God's justice—there was nothing he could do but wait prayerfully for the coming disaster . . . and for God's judgment to eventually fall on the wicked Babylonians as well. This passage is from the very end of Habakkuk's book, where he makes his way back from terror to joy.

> ¹⁶ I heard and my heart pounded,
>> my lips quivered at the sound;
> decay crept into my bones,
>> and my legs trembled.
> Yet I will wait patiently for the day of calamity
>> to come on the nation invading us.
> ¹⁷ Though the fig tree does not bud
>> and there are no grapes on the vines,
> though the olive crop fails
>> and the fields produce no food,
> though there are no sheep in the pen
>> and no cattle in the stalls,
> ¹⁸ yet I will rejoice in the LORD,
>> I will be joyful in God my Savior.
> ¹⁹ The Sovereign LORD is my strength;
>> he makes my feet like the feet of a deer,
>> he enables me to tread on the heights.

7. *Describe the circumstances that Habakkuk imagines will come upon Israel as a result of an enemy invasion. Why is it difficult to have joy in such circumstances?*

---

8. *What could enable people to rejoice in the Lord despite these circumstances?*

---

9. *Joy doesn't come to Habakkuk automatically. What emotions does he express (see verse 16)?*

---

10. *What enables Habakkuk to get to a place of settled joy (see verses 18–19)?*

---

11. *Are you able to have Habakkuk's attitude? Why did you answer the way you did?*

12. *Take two minutes of silence to reread the passage, looking for a sentence, phrase, or even one word that stands out as something Jesus may want you to focus on in your life. If you're meeting with a group, the leader will keep track of time. At the end of two minutes, you may share with the group the word or phrase that came to you in the silence.*

13. *Read the passage aloud again. Take another two minutes of silence, prayerfully considering what response God might want you to make to what you have read in His Word. If you're meeting with a group, the leader will again keep track of time. At the end of two minutes, you may share with the group what came to you in the silence if you wish.*

14. *If you're meeting with a group, how can the members pray for you? If you're using this study on your own, what would you like to say to God right now?*

LIVE IT

This week, each reading will focus on finding joy in the midst of circumstances, drawing from the wisdom and poetry found in Psalms. Read each passage slowly, pausing to think about what is being said. Rather than approaching this as an assignment to complete, think of it as an opportunity to meet with the One who loves you most. Use any of the questions that are helpful.

Day 1

Read Psalm 20:1–5. What are some of the blessings the psalmist asks God to shower on his hearers? Which ones stand out to you?

Joy is a natural response to victory (see verse 5). Do you think it is okay to pray for victory like this? Why or why not?

What helps you have joy even if the Lord doesn't grant all your requests (see verse 5)?

_____

_____

_____

Pray these blessings today for someone you care about.

Day 2

Read Psalm 47:1–9. What reasons for joy does this psalm celebrate?

_____

_____

_____

Why do you suppose singing is such an effective way to praise God and increase one's joy?

_____

_____

_____

What role does singing have in your life? Why? How could you build more of it into your life?

_____

_____

_____

_____

Go to a private place, shut the door, and sing praises to God. Don't worry if your voice isn't perfect!

Day 3

Read Psalm 65:5–8. What reasons for joy does this psalmist celebrate?

What are some of God's wonders that hold you in awe?

How does reflecting on the wonders of God help you to recognize His loving, constant control—regardless of the challenges you are facing?

Choose one of God's wonders today and spend some time praising Him for it.

Day 4

Read Psalm 65:9–13. For what does the psalmist rejoice in these verses?

Habakkuk was able to rejoice even while anticipating famine. Where are you today—rejoicing in abundance or rejoicing in spite of lacking something?

Sometimes a lack in one area can blind you to abundance in other areas. What are the areas of abundance in your life?

Thank God today for providing abundantly for you in so many areas of your life.

Day 5

Read Psalm 66:1–12. What events is the psalmist referring to in verses 5–6?

Why is it relevant for God's people to praise Him for these events, even many centuries later?

What are some things the psalmist says that the people of God can praise Him for, even during times of testing and trial (see verses 10–12)?

Do something decisive to express your joy today at what God is doing for you. Push yourself a little out of your comfort zone.

NOTES

1. Stephen Covey, A. Roger Merrill, and Rebecca Merrill, *First Things First* (New York: Free Press, 1996), 103.

JOY AND STRENGTH

CONSIDER IT

Charles Spurgeon was one of the leading preachers in nineteenth-century England. However, in spite of his great success, he struggled off and on with debilitating depression. He could do little about the physical causes of depression, but by grace he found that he could choose joy in the midst of it and rely on God's strength. In one sermon, Spurgeon noted:

> There is a marvelous medicinal power in joy. Most medicines are distasteful; but this, which is the best of all medicines, is sweet to the taste, and comforting to the heart. This blessed joy is very contagious. One dolorous spirit brings a kind of plague into the house; one person who is wretched seems to stop all the birds from singing wherever he goes . . . [But] the grace of joy is contagious. Holy joy will oil the wheels of your life's machinery. Holy joy will strengthen you for your daily labor. Holy joy will beautify you and give you an influence over the lives of others.[1]

In this session, we will look at the context of the well-known Bible verse, "The joy of the LORD is your strength" (Nehemiah 8:10). We will see how right Spurgeon was that joy is one of the best medicines available.

1. *What is an endeavor for which you need strength this week?*

_____

_____

_____

2. *Have you noticed any growth in joy over the past three weeks since you've started focusing on it in this study? Describe your experience.*

_____

_____

_____

EXPERIENCE IT

Strength and Joy are in My dwelling place. So the closer to Me you live, the stronger and more joyful you will be. Invite Me to permeate your moments with My Presence. This helps you view people from a positive perspective. Whenever you're around someone who irritates you, don't focus on that person's flaws. Instead, gaze at *Me* through the eyes of your heart, and those irritants will wash over you without harming you—or hurting others. Judging other people is a sinful snare that draws you away from Me. How much better it is to *be joyful in Me, your Savior!*

The more you focus on Me, the more I can strengthen you. In fact, *I am your Strength.* You can train your mind to stay aware of Me even when other things are demanding your attention. I created you with an amazing brain that is able to be conscious of several things at once. Create a permanent place for Me in your mind, and My Light will shine on all your moments.

—FROM *JESUS ALWAYS,* JANUARY 31

3. *Focusing on Jesus is a key to joy and strength. What are some habits that can help followers of Christ better focus on Him throughout the day?*

4. *What are some tactics you can employ to deal with people who irritate you?*

I am *your Strength*! When you begin a day feeling weak and weary, it's all right. Your weakness can be a reminder of your need for Me. Remember that I am with you continually—ready to help you as you go along your way. Take My hand in joyful trust, letting Me guide you and *strengthen you*. I delight in helping you, My child.

Whenever you feel inadequate for the task ahead, stop and think about your resources. I, *your Strength*, am infinite: I never run out of anything. So when you work in collaboration with Me, don't set limits on what you expect to accomplish. I will give you what you need to keep moving forward, step by step. You may not reach the goal as quickly as you'd like, but you will get there in my perfect timing. Refuse to be discouraged by delays or detours. Instead, trust that I know what I'm doing—and just take the next step. Perseverance and trust in Me make a potent combination!

—FROM *JESUS ALWAYS*, JANUARY 24

5. *Do you tend to view yourself as weak or strong? What makes you think that of yourself? What's the truth about your strength?*

_____

_____

_____

_____

6. *How do you think having joy in the Lord can help you trust Him more for strength?*

_____

_____

_____

_____

STUDY IT

Read Nehemiah 8:5–12. The Jewish people had spent seventy years in exile because of their disobedience to God's Law, but they were finally allowed to go back to their homeland. Jerusalem had been demolished, and so one of the first things the new governor, Nehemiah, did was to organize the rebuilding of the city wall. When the wall was finished, he and Ezra (the priest) brought the people together in Jerusalem to hear the reading of God's Word. Ezra stood on a platform and read it in Hebrew, and the Levites (members of the tribe of Levi, who were trained in God's Word) translated it into Aramaic, the language the people spoke.

⁵ Ezra opened the book. All the people could see him because he was standing above them; and as he opened it, the people all stood up.⁶ Ezra praised the LORD, the great God; and all the people lifted their hands and responded, "Amen! Amen!" Then they bowed down and worshiped the LORD with their faces to the ground.

⁷ The Levites—Jeshua, Bani, Sherebiah, Jamin, Akkub, Shabbethai, Hodiah, Maaseiah, Kelita, Azariah, Jozabad, Hanan and Pelaiah—instructed the people in the Law while the people were standing there.⁸ They read from the Book of the Law of God, making it clear and giving the meaning so that the people understood what was being read.

⁹ Then Nehemiah the governor, Ezra the priest and teacher of the Law, and the Levites who were instructing the people said to them all, "This day is holy to the LORD your God. Do not mourn or weep." For all the people had been weeping as they listened to the words of the Law.

¹⁰ Nehemiah said, "Go and enjoy choice food and sweet drinks, and send some to those who have nothing prepared. This day is holy to our Lord. Do not grieve, for the joy of the LORD is your strength."

¹¹ The Levites calmed all the people, saying, "Be still, for this is a holy day. Do not grieve."

¹² Then all the people went away to eat and drink, to send portions of food and to celebrate with great joy, because they now understood the words that had been made known to them.

7. What attitude toward God do the people express in verse 6? How can you tell?

8. Why do you think the people wept when they heard and understood God's Law (see verse 9)?

9. Why didn't Nehemiah want the people to grieve on this occasion (see verse 10)?

10. What do you think it means to have the joy of the Lord as one's strength?

11. What causes the people to celebrate with joy (see verse 12)? Does that same thing give you joy? Why or why not?

12. *Take two minutes of silence to reread the passage, looking for a sentence, phrase, or even one word that stands out as something Jesus may want you to focus on in your life. If you're meeting with a group, the leader will keep track of time. At the end of two minutes, you may share with the group the word or phrase that came to you in the silence.*

13. *Read the passage aloud again. Take another two minutes of silence, prayerfully considering what response God might want you to make to what you have read in His Word. If you're meeting with a group, the leader will again keep track of time. At the end of two minutes, you may share with the group what came to you in the silence if you wish.*

14. *If you're meeting with a group, how can the members pray for you? If you're using this study on your own, what would you like to say to God right now?*

LIVE IT

This week, each reading will focus on the joy of being strong in the Lord as told through the book of Psalms. Read each passage slowly, pausing to think about what is being said. Rather than approaching this as an assignment to complete, think of it as an opportunity to meet with the One who loves you most. Use any of the questions that are helpful.

Day 1

Read Psalm 68:1–6. How does the psalmist rejoice in God's strength in these verses?

What are some of God's traits that the psalmist points out (see verses 5–6)? How do these reveal His strength in every situation?

In verse 6, the psalmist writes, "God sets the lonely in families" and gives the desolate a homeland. How could God use you to be a source of strength for a lonely person?

Thank God today for being a willing Father to the fatherless. Turn to Him in faith with your own needs.

Day 2

Read Psalm 86:1–4. How does the psalmist describe himself in verse 1? What does he recognize about his power in relation to God's strength?

_____

_____

_____

How does the psalmist describe himself in verse 2? How does he know God will protect him?

_____

_____

_____

How can the psalmist find joy in the Lord in spite of his needs? What is required (see verse 4)?

_____

_____

_____

_____

Ask God to bring you joy during your day as you recognize your needs and your dependence on His strength. Be alert to how He responds to that prayer.

Day 3

Read Psalm 90:13–17. In this psalm, believed to be a prayer from Moses, what does the psalmist seek (see verses 13–16)? Can you identify with his longing? Why or why not?

What do you think "establish the work of our hands" means (verse 17)?

What does the psalmist say will give him joy? How does he recognize his dependence on God?

Talk with God about whatever is hard for you. Let Him be the person you rely on today.

Day 4

Read Psalm 92:4–15. What mighty deeds of the Lord make you glad (see verse 4)?

_____

_____

_____

_____

What are some of the Lord's great works that you have seen in your life (see verse 5)?

_____

_____

_____

_____

_____

How confident are you that "the righteous will flourish" (verse 12)? Is this something you know for certain, or do you have doubts? Explain.

_____

_____

_____

_____

_____

As you go through your day, keep turning your thoughts to God's mighty deeds.

Day 5

Read Psalm 147:2–6. This psalm was written after the exiles began to return to Jerusalem. What does the psalmist remind the people that God has done for them (see verses 2–3)?

_____

_____

_____

What does the psalmist say about God's power and knowledge (see verses 2–5)?

_____

_____

_____

What does the psalmist say the Lord does for those who humbly seek His strength (see verse 6)?

_____

_____

_____

Remind yourself of God's strength today, and let that feed your praise and joy in Him.

NOTES

1. Charles Spurgeon, Sermon no. 2405, delivered at the Metropolitan Tabernacle, Newington, March 20, 1887, *The Spurgeon Archive*, http://www.romans45.org/spurgeon/sermons/2405.htm.

JOY DESPITE FEAR

CONSIDER IT

Cyprian, a wealthy lawyer and senator in a prosperous city of the ancient Roman Empire, was about forty-five years old when he became a Christian sometime around AD 245. At the time, Christianity was an illegal and banned religion, and believers in Christ were being persecuted—especially in Cyprian's hometown of Carthage.

At one point, Cyprian was asked to explain why he had decided to convert to a faith that had put his life at stake. In reply, Cyprian penned a monologue as if to a friend (Donatus), in which he pointed out the many evils of his world: murder as a spectator sport in the amphitheaters, armies harrying defenseless civilians, robbers on land and pirates at sea. To conclude, he wrote:

> It is a bad world . . . but I have discovered in the midst of it a company of quiet and holy people who have learned a great secret. They have found a joy which is a thousand times better than any of the pleasures of our sinful life. They are despised and persecuted, but they care not: they are masters of their souls. They have overcome the world. These people, Donatus, are the Christians—and I am one of them.[1]

Just thirteen years later, Cyprian was beheaded for his faith. In this session, we will consider how Christian joy can coexist with the completely normal fears of life in a fallen world.

1. *What are some of the things that people are legitimately afraid of in this world?*

_____

_____

_____

_____

2. *Do you agree that Christians are "masters of their souls"? Why or why not?*

_____

_____

_____

_____

EXPERIENCE IT

It is possible for My followers to be joyful and afraid at the same time. When an angel told the women who came to My tomb that I had risen from the dead, they were *"afraid yet filled with joy."* So do not let fear keep you from experiencing the Joy of My Presence. It is not a luxury reserved for times when your problems—and the crises in the world—seem under control. My loving Presence is yours to enjoy today, tomorrow, and forever!

Do not give in to joyless living by letting worries about the present or the future weigh you down. Instead, remember that *neither the present nor the future, nor any powers, nor anything else in all creation, will be able to separate you from My Love.*

Talk with Me about your fears, expressing your thoughts and feelings freely. Relax in My Presence and entrust all your concerns to Me. Then ask Me to bless you with My Joy, which *no one can take from you.*

—FROM *JESUS ALWAYS*, JANUARY 6

3. *How would you describe the difference between fear and worry?*

_____

_____

_____

_____

4. *What are some truth-filled reminders that can help believers in Christ deal with fear?*

My ways are mysterious and unpredictable, but they are good. When you look at world events—with so much rampant evil—it's easy to feel fearful and discouraged. You cannot comprehend why I allow such cruelty and suffering. The difficulty lies in the fact that I am infinite and you are not. Many things are simply beyond your comprehension. But do not despair. When you reach the limits of your understanding, trusting Me will carry you onward. Affirm your *trust in Me* through silent and spoken prayers. Stay in communication with Me!

Don't get trapped in a posture of demanding to know "Why?" That is the wrong question to ask Me. The right questions are: "How do You want me to view this situation?" and "What do You want me to do right now?" You cannot change the past, so start with the present moment and seek to find My way forward. Trust Me one day, one moment, at a time. *Do not fear, for I am with you. I will strengthen you and help you.*

—From *Jesus Always*, March 9

5. *What are some tactics for dealing with fear of an uncertain future?*

---

6. *What could be wrong with asking God, "Why did you allow this?"*

_____

_____

_____

_____

STUDY IT

Read Matthew 28:1–10. To provide some context for this story, on the Friday afternoon when Jesus died, two of His followers put Him in a tomb that resembled a cave and rolled a stone over the opening. That evening the Sabbath began, and Sabbath laws forbade Jesus' followers from visiting the tomb. So, Sunday morning was the earliest the women could get there. Once the stone was rolled into place, it would have been much too heavy for the women to remove from the entrance. There were battle-hardened Roman soldiers guarding the tomb because the chief priests were concerned that someone might try to steal Jesus' body and spread a rumor about His rising from the dead.

¹ After the Sabbath, at dawn on the first day of the week, Mary Magdalene and the other Mary went to look at the tomb.

² There was a violent earthquake, for an angel of the Lord came down from heaven and, going to the tomb, rolled back the stone and sat on it. ³ His appearance was like lightning, and his clothes were white as snow. ⁴ The guards were so afraid of him that they shook and became like dead men.

⁵ The angel said to the women, "Do not be afraid, for I know that you are looking for Jesus, who was crucified. ⁶ He is not here; he has risen, just as he said. Come and see the place where he lay. ⁷ Then go quickly and tell his disciples: 'He has risen from the dead and is going ahead of you into Galilee. There you will see him.' Now I have told you."

⁸ So the women hurried away from the tomb, afraid yet filled with joy, and ran to tell his disciples. ⁹ Suddenly Jesus met them. "Greetings," he said. They came to him, clasped his feet and worshiped him. ¹⁰ Then Jesus said to them, "Do not be afraid. Go and tell my brothers to go to Galilee; there they will see me."

7. *Why were the women in this story afraid (see verse 8)?*

8. *How do you suppose it was possible for the women to be afraid yet filled with joy?*

9. *What is something wonderful that you could focus on in order to sustain joy even when there are scary things in your life?*

10. *Why do you suppose the women clasped Jesus' feet when they saw Him (see verse 9)?*

11. *What do you think was Jesus' intent when He told the women not to be afraid (see verse 10)? Why did you answer the way you did?*

12. *Take two minutes of silence to reread the passage, looking for a sentence, phrase, or even one word that stands out as something Jesus may want you to focus on in your life. If you're meeting with a group, the leader will keep track of time. At the end of two minutes, you may share with the group the word or phrase that came to you in the silence.*

13. *Read the passage aloud again. Take another two minutes of silence, prayerfully considering what response God might want you to make to what you have read in His Word. If you're meeting with a group, the leader will* *again keep track of time. At the end of two minutes, you may share with the group what came to you in the silence if you wish.*

---

14. *If you're meeting with a group, how can the members pray for you? If you're using this study on your own, what would you like to say to God right now?*

LIVE IT

This week, each reading will focus on finding joy in the midst of fear as portrayed in the book of Psalms. Read each passage slowly, pausing to think about what is being said. Rather than approaching this as an assignment to complete, think of it as an opportunity to meet with the One who loves you most. Use any of the questions that are helpful.

Day 1

Read Psalm 23:1–6. What are some fears that David identifies in this well-known psalm?

How does David reveal his joy in the Lord in spite of his fears?

What does it mean that God prepares "a table" before His children in the presence of their enemies (see verse 5)? What does this say about who or what you should fear if you belong to Him?

Thank God for His goodness today, even if you feel as though you are walking through a dark valley.

Day 2

Read Psalm 94:16–19. How did the Lord address fears in this psalmist's life?

Have you ever been consoled by the Lord? How did His consolation encourage you?

Do you struggle with fears of "the wicked" (verse 16)? If so, how? If not, what do you struggle with? What help do you need from the Lord?

If you are a child of God, cry out to God today about what you need from Him.

Day 3

Read Psalm 95:1–7. What does it mean to call God "the Rock of our salvation" (verse 1)? What does that imagery say about the power of God versus any fears a Christian may have?

Why is it helpful to remember that the depths and the heights of the world are all in God's hands (see verse 4)?

What is the point of bowing and kneeling when we are rejoicing in the Lord (see verse 6)? What do these postures express toward God even in fearful times?

Today, remember that God is the Rock of salvation for those who have accepted Him as their Lord. Turn to God rather than submitting to your fears.

Day 4

Read Psalm 96:7–13. What does it mean to "ascribe" something to the Lord?

How should it calm your fears to know that all creation rejoices before the Lord (see verse 13)?

Does it give you joy or fear to think of the Lord coming to "judge the world in righteousness" (verse 13)? Why did you answer the way you did?

Use this psalm today as a springboard for your own praise of God.

Day 5

Read Psalm 97:8–12. What causes Zion (the city of Jerusalem) and the surrounding villages of Judah to rejoice (see verse 8)? Why?

What promise is given to those who are faithful to the Lord (see verse 10)?

What does it mean to be righteous? Why would that give a person joy in spite of fear?

Ask God to show you today what it means to be righteous and to live that way.

NOTES

1. George Hodges, "Saints and Heroes to the End of the Middle Ages," *The Baldwin Project*, http://www.mainlesson.com/display.php?author=hodges&book=saints&story=Cyprian.

JOY AND HEALING

CONSIDER IT

Bennet Omalu is a Nigerian-born doctor and medical examiner who discovered a likely link between the concussions football players suffer and mental and mood disorders later in life. He discovered it while doing an autopsy on a former NFL player who died after suffering cognitive impairment, mental instability, drug abuse, and suicide attempts. The National Football League disputed Omalu's findings for seven years until finally, in 2009, its front office acknowledged the link. Omalu's story was dramatized in the 2015 film *Concussion*.

In one interview, Omalu said that a primary reason he cared about these football players was that he himself had struggled with depression as a teen and young adult. His gloom lasted throughout his medical training and nearly derailed his plan to be a doctor. It lifted only when he finally found a sense of purpose in doing autopsies to identify a person's cause of death.[1]

God doesn't promise anyone total physical and emotional healing in this life. But there's a reason why most of Jesus' miracles during His earthly ministry were healings, and why many of the psalms offer thanks for healing. God loves to heal people, and healing often leads to joy. In this session, we consider a psalm of thanks for healing to see what it can teach us about joy.

1. *When have you longed for healing from the Lord?*

_____

_____

_____

2. *When have you received healing from the Lord?*

_____

_____

_____

EXPERIENCE IT

A bruised reed I will not break, and a dimly burning wick I will not extinguish. I know you sometimes feel as weak and helpless as a bent reed or a faintly burning flame. Accept your weakness and brokenness, beloved; let them open your heart to Me. You can be fully yourself with Me because I understand you perfectly. As you tell Me your troubles, I refresh you and offer you *Peace that surpasses all comprehension.* Instead of trying to figure everything out, *lean on Me* in confident trust. Go off-duty for a while, trusting that I'm watching over you and working on your behalf.

My healing work within you is most effective when you are resting in My watchful care. Though the mountains be shaken and the hills be removed, yet My unfailing Love for you will not be shaken nor My covenant of Peace be removed—for I have compassion on you. Whenever you're feeling weak and wounded, come confidently into My Presence to receive abundant Love and Peace.

—FROM *JESUS ALWAYS*, SEPTEMBER 23

3. *Do you ever feel as weak and helpless as a bent reed or a faintly burning flame? If so, how do you usually deal with that feeling?*

_____

_____

_____

4. *How, in practice, do you rest in Jesus' watchful care if you've entrusted your life to Him?*

_____

_____

_____

I am a Shield for all who take refuge in Me. On some days you feel your need of My shielding Presence more than on other days. At times you're not even aware that you need protection, but I am continually close by—watching over you. I delight in being your Protector, so you can always find shelter in Me.

One of the best ways to make Me *your Refuge* is to spend focused time with Me and *pour out your heart to Me.* Tell Me about the things that have wounded you: the unfair things done to you or said about you. Trust that I care about you and want to heal your hurts. Also, I know the truth about everything; My view of you is untainted by innuendos and half-truths.

Knowing that I understand you completely is vital to your healing. It is also crucial for forgiving those who have wounded you. Forgiveness is usually a process, so keep at it till you are free. Rejoice in Me, beloved, for I came to *make you free.*

—From *Jesus Always*, April 24

5. *What helps you pour out your heart to the Lord about the areas in which you need healing? What hinders you?*

6. *In Psalm 139:1, David writes, "You have searched me, LORD, and you know me." Why is knowing that God understands you completely so important for emotional healing?*

Study It

Read Psalm 30:1–12. This is one of a handful of thanksgiving psalms. The psalmist (likely David) has been rescued by God from a serious illness. Before the illness, he was highly confident (see verse 6), but the illness refocused his attention on his complete dependence on God. The psalm shows a pattern—the psalmist was ill, he called on God, and God answered—and he repeats each of these elements for emphasis. As you read, note that *sackcloth* (see verse 11) was a coarse, rather itchy fabric used to make garments to express mourning. The *royal mountain* (see verse 7) is Mount Zion, where the king's palace stood in Jerusalem.

¹ I will exalt you, LORD,

    for you lifted me out of the depths

    and did not let my enemies gloat over me.

² LORD my God, I called to you for help,

    and you healed me.

³ You, LORD, brought me up from the realm of the dead;

    you spared me from going down to the pit.

⁴ Sing the praises of the LORD, you his faithful people;

    praise his holy name.

⁵ For his anger lasts only a moment,

    but his favor lasts a lifetime;

weeping may stay for the night,

    but rejoicing comes in the morning.

⁶ When I felt secure, I said,

    "I will never be shaken."

⁷ LORD, when you favored me,

    you made my royal mountain stand firm;

but when you hid your face,

    I was dismayed.

⁸ To you, LORD, I called;

    to the Lord I cried for mercy:

⁹ "What is gained if I am silenced,
  if I go down to the pit?
Will the dust praise you?
  Will it proclaim your faithfulness?
¹⁰ Hear, LORD, and be merciful to me;
  LORD, be my help."
¹¹ You turned my wailing into dancing;
  you removed my sackcloth and clothed me with joy,
¹² that my heart may sing your praises and not be silent.
  LORD my God, I will praise you forever.

7. *In verse 2, the psalmist writes, "LORD my God, I called to you for help, and you healed me." What is the benefit even if God does not heal you immediately?*

_____

_____

_____

8. *What if you call out to the Lord and He doesn't heal you at all? Can we still have joy?*

_____

_____

_____

9. *In verses 9 and 10, we read some of the things the psalmist prayed when he asked for healing. What does he say? Does any of it surprise you? Explain your response.*

_____

_____

_____

10. *How does the psalmist describe his joy in verse 11? Do you ever have joy like that?*

----

11. *In what aspect of your life do you need the Lord's mercy today?*

----

12. *Take two minutes of silence to reread the passage, looking for a sentence, phrase, or even one word that stands out as something Jesus may want you to focus on in your life. If you're meeting with a group, the leader will keep track of time. At the end of two minutes, you may share with the group the word or phrase that came to you in the silence.*

----

13. *Read the passage aloud again. Take another two minutes of silence, prayerfully considering what response God might want you to make to what you have read in His Word. If you're meeting with a group, the leader will* *again keep track of time. At the end of two minutes, you may share with the group what came to you in the silence if you wish.*

_____

_____

_____

14. *If you're meeting with a group, how can the members pray for you? If you're using this study on your own, what would you like to say to God right now?*

_____

_____

_____

LIVE IT

This week, each reading will focus on prayers and praise to God for healing as found in the book of Psalms. Read each passage slowly, pausing to think about what is being said. Rather than approaching this as an assignment to complete, think of it as an opportunity to meet with the One who loves you most. Use any of the questions that are helpful.

Day 1

Read Psalm 6:1–5. How does the psalmist describe his condition (see verses 2–3)?

_____

_____

_____

How does the psalmist express his impatience to God? When have you had a similar reaction when waiting for God to answer?

_____

_____

_____

What "argument" does the psalmist make as to why God should restore him (see verse 5)?

_____

_____

_____

Today, share with God exactly how you are feeling and what you would like for Him to do in your life, and then entrust yourself to Him in faith.

Day 2

Read Psalm 91:1–6. What does the psalmist say about finding rest in the Lord (see verses 1–2)?

_____

_____

_____

How does the psalmist express his trust in God to preserve his life (see verses 2–4)?

_____

_____

_____

In what ways do you need God to give you refuge today?

_____

_____

_____

Ask the Lord to provide a safe place for you in times of weakness and illness, and express your joy to Him for offering to be your refuge.

Day 3

Read Psalm 103:1–5. What does it mean to praise God with your "inmost being" (verse 1)?

_____

_____

_____

What are some of the benefits from God that the psalmist names (see verses 2–4)?

_____

_____

_____

When has God renewed your strength "like the eagle's" (verse 5)?

_____

_____

_____

_____

Today, thank God for all the simple benefits He provides—including your life and health.

Day 4

Read Psalm 107:17–22. What caused some of the people the psalmist describes to suffer afflictions? What did they do as a result (see verses 17–19)?

How did the Lord respond to them? What does this say about God (see verses 19–20)?

As in Psalm 30, joy is the sensible response to healing (see verse 22). Why do you suppose many people forget to express prayers of joy and gratitude to the Lord when they are healed?

Write down three things for which you are thankful today and express them to God.

Day 5

Read Psalm 118:15–19. Why do you suppose the righteous shout for joy (see verse 15)?

For what is the psalmist thankful in verse 17? Do you share his sentiments? Why or why not?

How does the psalmist express his gratitude to God in spite of his afflictions (see verse 18)?

Today, proclaim some of the good things that the Lord has done. Who could you tell?

NOTES

Bennet Omalu, "The Doctor Who Discovered the Dangers of Concussions in Football," *Guideposts*, August 7, 2017, https://www.guideposts.org/better-living/life-advice/finding-life-purpose/the-doctor-who-discovered-the-dangers-of-concussions.

JOY IN SINGING

CONSIDER IT

Martin Rinkart was a pastor in Germany when the Thirty Years' War broke out in 1617. His city, Eilenburg, had a wall around it, so it became a magnet for refugees. The overcrowding led to food shortages and an outbreak of plague by 1637. One of the city's four pastors ran away, and two others died, so Rinkart was left as the sole pastor, performing dozens of funerals each day. One of those was for his wife.

At one point, the Swedish army besieged the city for months, promising to leave only if the people paid an impossible ransom. Rinkart begged for a lower amount, but the Swedes insisted. Rinkart knelt and prayed so passionately that the Swedish officer was moved to settle for the lesser ransom. When peace finally looked likely, Rinkart wrote a hymn for his children to sing at the dinner table, *"Nun danket alle Gott,"* which was later translated into English as "Now Thank We All Our God":

> Now thank we all our God
> With heart and hands and voices
> Who wondrous things has done
> In whom this world rejoices

Although Rinkart was barely able to feed his children, he wanted them to grow up rejoicing in God because they had life. In this session, we will consider the special role singing has in sustaining a joy-filled life.

1. *What role does singing play in your worship?*

_____

_____

_____

_____

_____

2. *What are some favorite praise songs and hymns that you like to sing? Why are those particular songs meaningful to you?*

EXPERIENCE IT

Glory in My holy Name; let the hearts of those who seek Me rejoice. To "glory" in something is to give it praise and honor. Jesus is *the Name that is above every name*—it represents *Me* in all My sinless perfection. As My follower, you can whisper, speak, or sing My Name with confidence that I am listening. This draws you closer to Me and helps you find strength in My Presence. It also serves to drive away your spiritual enemies.

I'm delighted that you take time to seek Me, desiring to know Me better. Come freely into My loving Presence, letting your heart *rejoice in Me.* Remember that you are on *holy ground*, and breathe in the rarified air of My holiness. Release cares and concerns while you rest in the splendor of My Glory. Let My joyous Presence envelop you— permeating you through and through. As you delight in My nearness, time seems to slow down, enhancing your enjoyment of Me. Thank Me for these moments of sweet intimacy.

—FROM *JESUS ALWAYS*, FEBRUARY 3

3. *What are some reasons a Christian can sing Jesus' name with confidence?*

4. *If you are a follower of Christ, how are you doing at making daily time to rejoice in His presence? What helps you?*

_____

_____

_____

_____

Sing for Joy to Me, your Strength. Christmas music is one of the best blessings of the season, and it doesn't have to cost you anything. You can sing the carols at church or in the privacy of your home—or even in your car. As you are making a joyful noise, pay close attention to the words. They are all about Me and My miraculous entrance into your world through the virgin birth. Singing from your heart increases both your Joy and your energy. It also blesses Me.

I created you to glorify Me and enjoy Me forever. So it's not surprising that you feel more fully alive when you glorify Me through song. I want you to learn to enjoy Me in more and more aspects of your life. Before you arise from your bed each morning, try to become aware of My Presence with you. Say to yourself: *"Surely the Lord is in this place."* This will awaken your awareness to the wonders of My continual nearness. *I will fill you with Joy in My Presence.*

—From *Jesus Always*, December 17

5. *What are some Christmas carols that you especially like? Why do you like those songs?*

_____

_____

_____

_____

6. *How do you respond to the idea of feeling more fully alive when you glorify God through song? Has this been true of you? Why or why not?*

STUDY IT

Read 1 Chronicles 16:23–33. King David wrote this psalm to give thanks to the Lord. David had defeated Israel's enemies in battle, bringing peace to the nation. He had built a palace for himself in Jerusalem, and now he set up God's royal tent (the tabernacle) on the site in Jerusalem where his son would one day build a temple for God. Members of the tribe of Levi carried the ark of the covenant (a chest that contained holy objects and represented God's throne among His people) into Jerusalem and placed it in the holy tent. This was the event that David was celebrating in song.

> ²³ Sing to the LORD, all the earth;
>> proclaim his salvation day after day.
> ²⁴ Declare his glory among the nations,
>> his marvelous deeds among all peoples.
> ²⁵ For great is the LORD and most worthy of praise;
>> he is to be feared above all gods.
> ²⁶ For all the gods of the nations are idols,
>> but the LORD made the heavens.
> ²⁷ Splendor and majesty are before him;
>> strength and joy are in his dwelling place.
> ²⁸ Ascribe to the LORD, all you families of nations,
>> ascribe to the LORD glory and strength.
> ²⁹ Ascribe to the LORD the glory due his name;
>> bring an offering and come before him.

Worship the LORD in the splendor
  of his holiness.
³⁰ Tremble before him, all the earth!
  The world is firmly established; it cannot be moved.
³¹ Let the heavens rejoice, let the earth be glad;
  let them say among the nations, "The LORD reigns!"
³² Let the sea resound, and all that is in it;
  let the fields be jubilant, and everything in them!
³³ Let the trees of the forest sing,
    let them sing for joy before the LORD,
    for he comes to judge the earth.

7. *In this psalm, David calls on the whole earth to sing to the Lord (see verse 23), including the trees and the sea (see verses 32–33). How does nature do this?*

8. *What are some of the things that David wanted the whole earth to sing about?*

9. *How does this psalm express and inspire joy?*

10. *When David says, "Let the sea resound, and all that is in it" (verse 32),
how do you imagine the sea resounding with music?*

_____

_____

_____

11. *How has your attitude toward singing been affected by discussing this
psalm and the readings? How could you better incorporate singing into your
life and worship of God?*

_____

_____

_____

12. *Take two minutes of silence to reread the passage, looking for a sentence,
phrase, or even one word that stands out as something Jesus may want you to
focus on in your life. If you're meeting with a group, the leader will keep track
of time. At the end of two minutes, you may share with the group the word or
phrase that came to you in the silence.*

_____

_____

_____

13. *Read the passage aloud again. Take another two minutes of silence,
prayerfully considering what response God might want you to make to what*

you have read in His Word. If you're meeting with a group, the leader will again keep track of time. At the end of two minutes, you may share with the group what came to you in the silence if you wish.

_____

_____

_____

14. *If you're meeting with a group, how can the members pray for you? If you're using this study on your own, what would you like to say to God right now?*

_____

_____

_____

LIVE IT

This week, each reading will focus on joy expressed through singing as portrayed in the book of Psalms. Read each passage slowly, pausing to think about what is being said. Rather than approaching this as an assignment to complete, think of it as an opportunity to meet with the One who loves you most. Use any of the questions that are helpful.

Day 1

Read Psalm 126:1–6. What does it mean to say, "Those who sow with tears will reap with songs of joy" (verse 5)?

_____

_____

_____

In what ways does the Lord restore the fortunes of His children?

_____

_____

_____

What restoration are you praying for now?

_____

_____

_____

Even if you are in a season of tears, thank God that He will one day restore those who choose to follow Him and pursue His ways with songs of joy.

Day 2

Read Psalm 132:13–16. Why will the faithful ones in Zion sing for joy?

_____

_____

_____

What does it mean that God will make Zion His "resting place for ever and ever" (verse 14)? How does that promise apply to a believer's life?

_____

_____

_____

How has the Lord demonstrated that He has chosen those who follow Him?

Sing for joy to the Lord today and thank Him for His promise to always be with His children.

Day 3

Read Psalm 137:1–6. Does it help you to know there are times for weeping when songs of joy are temporarily set aside? Why or why not?

What reasons for weeping does this psalmist express?

Is this psalmist right to consider Jerusalem, the site of God's house, as his highest joy (see verse 6)? What do you think he means by this statement? Explain.

Today, look for ways to sing praises to God and thank Him that the times of weeping will end for those who choose to serve Him.

Day 4

Read Psalm 145:1–8. Why is the Lord worthy of praise according to this psalmist?

_____

_____

_____

_____

What does the psalmist want future generations to remember?

_____

_____

_____

_____

How can followers of God "joyfully sing of [His] righteousness" (verse 7)?

_____

_____

_____

_____

_____

Turn your answers to these questions into a prayer of joyful praise.

Day 5

Read Psalm 149:1–9. Why is the Lord worthy of new songs (see verse 1)?

_____

_____

_____

What should be the place of old songs, such as the psalms, in the life of the Lord's worshipers?

_____

_____

_____

Why do you suppose the psalmist speaks of singing for joy on our beds (see verse 5)? What does this say about the times and places that you can choose to worship the Lord?

_____

_____

_____

Sing to the Lord a new song today or an old one—but in all things praise the Lord.

JOY EVEN IN SUFFERING

CONSIDER IT

A woman named Jennifer, as a result of a stroke, has locked-in syndrome. Her conscious mind is fully intact, but she is unable to control any part of her body except for moving her eyes and blinking her eyelids. Her mother, Andrea, cares for Jennifer and Jennifer's two-year-old daughter while Jennifer's husband goes to work to pay for the many things that they need. Jennifer could easily despair of her limited life, but she and Andrea both insist they live with joy. Asked what keeps her going, Jennifer blinks her eyes to slowly spell out the word G-O-D.

We live in a world surrounded by suffering. Hurricanes, earthquakes, and fires can sweep away everything we own in minutes. Illnesses or accidents or other people's crimes can have devastating consequences. Friends or family members can walk out on us. Only the joy of a robust faith in God can withstand whatever life throws at us.

In this session, we will consider a night when the apostle Paul displayed extraordinary joy during a time of suffering. For Paul, the message he carried about Jesus was such good news that nothing anyone did to him could defeat his determination to praise God.

1. *What was one of the hardest times in your life? Summarize the situation briefly.*

2. *How did you keep going during that difficult time?*

EXPERIENCE IT

Let *My consolation*—My comfort—*bring Joy to your soul.* When anxiety is welling up within you, come to Me and *pour out your heart.* Then sit quietly in My Presence while I comfort you, helping you see things from My perspective. I remind you of your heavenly destination, for you are indeed on your way to Glory! I infuse My Joy and Peace into your heart, mind, and soul.

When you are joyful, this changes the way you view the world around you. Even though you see much darkness, you can also see the Light of My Presence continuing to shine. Moreover, the Joy in your soul gives you buoyancy, enabling you to rise above the countless problems in your life. Once you have gained this perspective, you will discover that you can comfort others in the midst of their troubles. They will find in you the consolation that you have found in Me. Thus your Joy becomes contagious, "infecting" those around you with Joy in *their* souls!

—FROM *JESUS ALWAYS,* JANUARY 5

3. *How would you describe a "fruitful" response to anxiety?*

_____

_____

_____

4. *As you near the end of this study, is the joy of the Lord still hard for you to experience, or is it giving you a kind of buoyancy with which to rise above life's problems? Explain.*

_____

_____

_____

I am the Joy that no one can take away from you. Savor the wonders of this gift, spending ample time in My Presence. Rejoice that this blessing is yours—I am yours—for all eternity!

Many things in this world can bring you pleasure for a while, but they are all passing away because of death and decay. In Me you have a matchless Treasure—Joy in the One who is *the same yesterday, today, and forever.* No one can take this pleasure away from you, for I am faithful and I never change.

Whenever you feel joyless, the problem is not in the Source (Me) but in the receiver. You may be so focused on other things—either pleasures or difficulties in your life—that you're neglecting your relationship with Me. The remedy is twofold: Remember that I am your *First Love*, and seek to put Me first in your life. Also, ask Me to increase your receptivity to My Presence. *Delight yourself in Me*, beloved, and receive Joy in full measure.

—From *Jesus Always*, January 23

5. *Why is God a more reliable source of joy than any person or thing in this life?*

_____

_____

_____

_____

6. *When you take time with God, are you aware of His presence? Or does it feel like He is absent? How reliable are these feelings?*

_____

_____

_____

_____

STUDY IT

Read Acts 16:16–34. These events took place in the city of Philippi in what is now northern Greece. This was the apostle Paul's first visit to Philippi, and the citizens of the town were generally hostile toward Jews—and toward Paul's team in particular. Many of the citizens were retired Roman soldiers. The "place of prayer" mentioned in verse 16 was a location outside the town walls where the few Jews in Philippi gathered to worship God. There was no Jewish synagogue inside the town. Luke, the writer of Acts, was apparently part of Paul's team at this point in the journey, which is why he wrote using the term "we."

[16] Once when we were going to the place of prayer, we were met by a female slave who had a spirit by which she predicted the future. She earned a great deal of money for her owners by fortune-telling. [17] She followed Paul and the rest of us, shouting, "These men are servants of the Most High God, who are telling you the way to be saved." [18] She kept this up for many days. Finally Paul became so annoyed that he turned around and said to the spirit, "In the name of Jesus Christ I command you to come out of her!" At that moment the spirit left her.

[19] When her owners realized that their hope of making money was gone, they seized Paul and Silas and dragged them into the marketplace to face the authorities. [20] They brought them before the magistrates and said, "These men are Jews, and are throwing our city into an uproar [21] by advocating customs unlawful for us Romans to accept or practice."

[22] The crowd joined in the attack against Paul and Silas, and the magistrates ordered them to be stripped and beaten with rods. [23] After they had been severely flogged, they were thrown into prison, and the jailer was commanded to guard them carefully. [24] When he received these orders, he put them in the inner cell and fastened their feet in the stocks.

[25] About midnight Paul and Silas were praying and singing hymns to God, and the other prisoners were listening to them. [26] Suddenly

there was such a violent earthquake that the foundations of the prison were shaken. At once all the prison doors flew open, and everyone's chains came loose. [27] The jailer woke up, and when he saw the prison doors open, he drew his sword and was about to kill himself because he thought the prisoners had escaped. [28] But Paul shouted, "Don't harm yourself! We are all here!"

[29] The jailer called for lights, rushed in and fell trembling before Paul and Silas. [30] He then brought them out and asked, "Sirs, what must I do to be saved?"

[31] They replied, "Believe in the Lord Jesus, and you will be saved— you and your household." [32] Then they spoke the word of the Lord to him and to all the others in his house. [33] At that hour of the night the jailer took them and washed their wounds; then immediately he and all his household were baptized. [34] The jailer brought them into his house and set a meal before them; he was filled with joy because he had come to believe in God—he and his whole household.

7. *What were the particular hardships that Paul and Silas suffered in Philippi (see verses 22–24)?*

_____

_____

_____

_____

8. *Why do you think Paul and Silas responded to their situation by praying aloud and singing hymns to God (see verse 25)?*

_____

_____

_____

9. *Think about this story from the jailer's viewpoint. What did he see, hear, and experience?*

10. *What if there had been no earthquake or any miraculous intervention of God into these circumstances? Would Paul and Silas's joy have been pointless? Explain.*

11. *What do you think you are meant to learn from this story?*

12. *Take two minutes of silence to reread the passage, looking for a sentence, phrase, or even one word that stands out as something Jesus may want you to focus on in your life. If you're meeting with a group, the leader will keep track of time. At the end of two minutes, you may share with the group the word or phrase that came to you in the silence.*

13. *Read the passage aloud again. Take another two minutes of silence, prayerfully considering what response God might want you to make to what you have read in His Word. If you're meeting with a group, the leader will again keep track of time. At the end of two minutes, you may share with the group what came to you in the silence if you wish.*

---

14. *If you're meeting with a group, how can the members pray for you? If you're using this study on your own, what would you like to say to God right now?*

LIVE IT

This week, each reading will focus on joy even in suffering as portrayed in the book of Psalms. Read each passage slowly, pausing to think about what is being said. Rather than approaching this as an assignment to complete, think of it as an opportunity to meet with the One who loves you most. Use any of the questions that are helpful.

Day 1

Read Psalm 5:8–12. It is believed that David wrote this psalm after being betrayed by his son Absalom and being forced to flee Jerusalem (see 2 Samuel

17). What is his prayer in verses 8–9?

What does David want God to do about his enemies (see verse 10)?

How does David express his joy in God's deliverance even though he has not yet been relieved of his suffering (see verses 11–12)?

Talk with God today about those who come against you. Hand them over to Him—you do not have to battle them by yourself any longer.

Day 2

Read Psalm 21:1–7. David likely wrote this psalm when he went to war against the Ammonites and Syrians (see 2 Samuel 10). Do you think David's words here are about joy when things are going well, or joy when things aren't going well?

Why is it important to give God credit for the things that He does for us even in the midst of trials and an uncertain future?

_____

_____

_____

_____

What are some of the things that make you joyful? Do you tend to give God credit for them? Why or why not?

_____

_____

_____

_____

Identify a victory in your life, give God the credit, and allow it to feed your joy.

Day 3

Read Psalm 22:1–10. David certainly wrote this psalm during a season of great danger and deprivation—things he experienced frequently on his way to assuming the throne. What is his initial complaint to God (see verses 1–2)? But what does he realize (see verses 3–5)?

_____

_____

_____

_____

How would you describe David's sufferings based on verses 6–8? How does David remind himself that even during these times, God is faithful (see verses 9–10)?

Read Matthew 27:45–46. Why do you think Jesus quoted this psalm during His final minutes on the cross? What was He expressing in that moment?

Take some time this day to reflect on what you know to be true about God's love and faithfulness. Ask Him to make His presence known to you in your situation.

Day 4

Read Psalm 57:4–11. It is believed that David wrote this psalm when he was on the run from King Saul and hiding in caves (see 1 Samuel 24). How does David describe his situation in this instance (see verse 4)?

What reason does David find to praise God even in these circumstances (see verses 5–6)?

_____

_____

_____

_____

What does David resolve to do while he is in hiding for his life (see verses 7–11)?

_____

_____

_____

_____

Today, resolve in your heart to somehow praise God in the midst of your trials.

Day 5

Read Psalm 119:49–56. The author of this psalm (the longest in the Bible) is unknown, but tradition holds that it was penned by either David, Ezra, or Daniel. Each of these men suffered serious hardship during their lives. What does the psalmist say gives him comfort (see verses 49–50)?

_____

_____

_____

_____

This psalmist finds joy in remembering God's laws (see verses 51–52). Why would someone find joy in God's commands during times of difficulty?

_____

_____

_____

_____

How has God's Word helped you personally during painful times in your life?

_____

_____

_____

_____

Seek God in His Word as you encounter challenges today.

LEADER'S NOTES

Thank you for your willingness to lead a group through this *Jesus Always* study. The rewards of leading are different from the rewards of participating, and we hope you find your own walk with Jesus deepened by this experience. In many ways, your group meeting will be structured like other Bible studies in which you've participated. You'll want to open in prayer, for example, and ask people to silence their phones. These leader's notes will focus on elements of the study that may be new to you.

CONSIDER IT

This first portion of the study functions as an icebreaker. It gets the group members thinking about the topic at hand by asking them to share from their own experience. Some people may be tempted to tell a long story in response to one of these questions, but the goal is to keep the answers brief. Ideally, you want everyone in the group to have a chance to answer the *Consider It* questions, so you may want to say up front that everyone needs to limit his or her answer to one minute.

With the rest of the study, it is generally not a good idea to go around the circle and have everyone answer every question—a free-flowing discussion is more desirable. But with the *Consider It* questions, you can go around the circle. Encourage shy people to share, but don't force them. Tell the group they should feel free to pass if they prefer not to answer a question.

EXPERIENCE IT

This is the group's chance to talk about excerpts from the *Jesus Always* devotional. You will need to monitor this discussion closely so that you have enough time for the actual study of God's Word that follows. If the group has a long and rich discussion on one of the devotional excerpts, you may choose to skip the other one and move on to the Bible study. Don't feel obliged to cover every *Experience It* question if the conversation is fruitful. On the other hand, do move on if the group gets off on a tangent.

STUDY IT

Try to do the *Study It* exercise in session 1 on your own before the group meets the first time so you can coach people on what to expect. Note that this section may be a little different from Bible studies your group has done in the past. The group will talk about the Bible passage as usual, but then there will be several minutes of silence so individuals can pray about what God might want to say to them personally through the reading. It will be up to you to keep track of the time and call people back to the discussion when the time is up. (There are some good timer apps that play a gentle chime or other pleasant sound instead of a disruptive noise.) If members aren't used to being silent in a group, brief them on what to expect.

Don't be afraid to let people sit in silence. Two minutes of quiet may seem like a long time at first, but it will help to train group members to sit in silence with God when they are alone. They can remain where they are in the circle, or if you have space, you can let them go off by themselves to other rooms at your instruction. If your group meets in a home, ask the host before the meeting which rooms are available for use. Some people will be more comfortable in the quiet if they have a bit of space from others.

When the group reconvenes after the time of silence, invite them to share what they experienced. There are several questions provided in this study guide that you can ask. Note that it's not necessary to cover every question if the group has a good discussion going. It's also not necessary to go around the circle and make everyone share.

Don't be concerned if the group members are reserved and slow to share after the exercise. People are often quiet when they are pulling together their ideas, and the exercise will have been a new experience for many of them. Just ask a question and let it hang in the air until someone speaks up. You can then say, "Thank you. What about others? What came to you when you sat with the passage?"

Some people may say they found it hard to quiet their minds enough to focus on the passage for those few minutes. Tell them this is okay. They are practicing a skill, and sometimes skills take time to learn. If they learn to sit quietly with God's Word in a group, they will become much more comfortable sitting with the Word on their own. Remind them that spending time in the Bible each day is one of the most valuable things they can do as believers in Christ.

PREPARATION

It's not necessary for group members to prepare anything for the study ahead of time. However, at the end of each study are five days' worth of suggestions for spending time in God's Word during the next week. These daily times are optional but valuable, so encourage the group to do them. Also, invite them to bring their questions and insights to the group at your next meeting, especially if they had a breakthrough moment or if they didn't understand something.

As the leader, there are a few things you should do to prepare for each meeting:

- *Read through the session.* This will help you become familiar with the content and know how to structure the discussion times.

- *Spend five to ten minutes doing the* Study It *questions on your own.* When the group meets, you'll be watching the clock, so you'll probably have a more fulfilling time with the passage if you do the exercise ahead of time. You can then spend time in the passage again with the group. This way, you'll be sure to have the key verses for that session deeply in your mind.

- *Pray for your group.* Pray especially that God will guide them in how to embrace the love that Jesus has demonstrated for them and, in turn, share that love with others in their world who need to experience it.

- *Bring extra supplies to your meeting.* Group members should bring their own pens for writing notes on the Bible reflection, but it is a good idea to have extras available for those who forget. You may also want to bring paper and Bibles for those who may have neglected to bring their study guides to the meeting.

Below you will find suggested answers for some of the study questions. Note that in many cases there is no one right answer, especially when the group members are sharing their personal experiences.

Session 1: Joy in Salvation

1. *Answers will vary. It might have been getting a new toy or seeing a best friend or getting to eat ice cream. This is a chance for the group to get to know each other better while thinking about what joy means to them. Childlike happiness is only an echo of joy, but hopefully it will get the group in touch with the simple things that sparked happiness when they were young.*

2. *This could be touchier territory, as things that robbed us of joy in our youth can continue to play a role in our hearts as adults without us even recognizing the extent. For instance, not getting our way may have robbed us of joy as children, but it's possible it still might have that same effect on us now if we haven't yielded "our way" to God. Or if our parents' fighting robbed us of joy in our childhood, we might still be living with that half-forgotten heartache.*

3. *There are many ways to refuse to allow adversity to keep us from enjoying God. For example, we can choose to persist in daily time with God even when life is hard, scheduling it in as a priority. We can choose to sing a song of praise to God even when something didn't go our way. We can opt to pray for someone who cuts us off in traffic instead of getting angry. And rather than dwelling on our complaints, we can decide to write down at least five things we are thankful for every day.*

4. *Many believers in Christ have only a vague notion of what they're looking forward to when it comes to the promises in God's Word about heaven. Eternal life is not just an unending church service—it's intimacy with the most beautiful, true, and holy Person who ever existed. It's a resurrected physical life that doesn't grow weak or decay, with joyous, purposeful work to do in service to God (see 1 Corinthians 15:35–58). It's also the ultimate reunion with loved ones.*

5. *The joy that followers of Christ experience is so much more than just an elevated mood. It's a deeply settled sense of well-being and peace that rests in their souls. This peace doesn't come and go with a believer's emotions—which are inevitably up and down. It's also not tied to circumstances.*

6. *Followers of Christ recognize that Jesus died in our place. We deserved the death penalty for treason against God, but Jesus volunteered to take that penalty on Himself so that God's justice could be satisfied and we could still have life. Jesus endured the terrible torment of our sins on the cross so that we might be free of them. This is why Christians have such cause to rejoice: because God offers the incredible gift of being free from the burden of our sins and dwelling with Him in heaven one day.*

7. *For followers of Christ, our living hope is eternal life with God, where death and pain and tears no longer exist. Even more, we're anticipating our own resurrection to new life in glorified (perfected and eternal) bodies. Jesus' resurrection is a promise that these things will come to pass. Biblical hope isn't wishful thinking but confident expectation. New birth in Christ is a down payment on a future life in resurrected bodies that dwell in the full presence of God.*

8. *Answers will vary. Some believers in Christ might be especially glad that their inheritance can never perish, spoil, or fade. Some might look forward to seeing the beauty of God—which would overwhelm them if they glimpsed it now. Some may look forward to the intimate relationships with God and with His people. Some may want to be caught up in worship, while others will delight in seeing lost loved ones.*

9. *The inheritance is guaranteed for faith-filled followers of Jesus. It is not guaranteed for anyone else. Staying connected to Jesus through faith—in who He is and what He has done for us—is a crucial step. This isn't faith in faith; it's faith in Christ and His redemption for sin.*

10. *Trials test a believer's faith and prove it to be genuine. Anybody can have "faith" when everything is going well, but to continue to trust Jesus when life is hard requires the "gold standard" of true faith. As Christians, when trials come we can remember that though things are hard now, we can look forward to an "inexpressible joy" in Christ.*

11. *Answers will vary. Simply taking the time to consciously reflect on the grace that Jesus has shown in saving His own from sin can help us learn to appreciate the depths of what He has done. As Paul wrote, "While we were still sinners, Christ died for us" (Romans 5:8). Christ didn't wait for us to come to Him—He actively seeks out those who will believe in Him. It's crucial to not allow the business and worries of the day to distract us as His followers from this reality. We need to take time to be with God each day so that our love for Him can be nurtured.*

12. *Answers will vary. It's fine for this process to be unfamiliar to the group at first. Be sure to keep track of time.*

13. *Answers will vary. Note that some people may find the silence intimidating at first. Their anxiety might tempt them to fill the air with noise, but it will be helpful for these group members to just take a quiet moment before God. Let them express their discomfort once you're all gathered together again, but make sure it is balanced by those who found the silence strengthening. Helping people become comfortable with this "holy quiet" will serve their private daily times with God in wonderful ways.*

14. *Take as much time as you can to pray for each other. You might have someone write down the prayer requests so you can keep track of answers to prayer.*

Session 2: Joy in Restoration

1. *For some group members, Easter may have been about chocolate bunnies and egg hunts and a big family dinner. Or Easter may have gone by as just another day. For others, celebrating Christ's resurrection may have been part of the day.*

2. *Answers will vary. Some people may feel the same about Easter today as they did when they were growing up—it was just another holiday on the calendar. But others, especially followers in Christ, will recognize the deep significance of Easter and be reminded of the hope it holds for them. The point of this question is to get the group thinking about how the resurrection has or hasn't been something prominent in their minds.*

3. *Some group members may have seen paintings or films that depicted the risen Jesus. They may have a mental picture of Him alive, seated at the right hand of God the Father (see Colossians 3:1). They may feel joyful when they consider the risen Christ, or they may have an absence of joy—even apathy—because they haven't yet recognized the depth of the sacrifice that He went through to be restored to them.*

4. *Jesus' offer to be with us now and forever will only evoke joy within us if we have accepted His offer! What's more, even if we have accepted Him as Lord and Savior, we need to spend enough time with Him in prayer each day to cultivate a "living awareness" of His presence. Jesus really does offer to be with us, but it's easy for us to get too busy or preoccupied to be aware of Him. We Christians need to pause throughout each day and remind ourselves, "Jesus, You have promised to be with me."*

5. *Some group members may immediately get a jolt of happiness just from saying those words. Others will have little response and may need to cultivate the truth of this statement by repeating it or by exploring what keeps them from experiencing this as a real truth. Once again, to personally know the joy of God's reconciliation through the cross, we must take the step of accepting Christ's offer of salvation and make Him the Lord of our lives.*

6. *It's normal for followers of Christ who are just beginning the practice of disciplining their thoughts to find that their minds wander when they try to focus on God. The key is to remain calm and keep shifting our thoughts back to God when they stray. We can repeat a short passage of Scripture* *to ourselves, or just say a phrase like, "Jesus, You are my joy." Immersing ourselves in God's Word can also fix our thoughts on God more often.*

7. *Jesus convinces His followers by telling them to touch Him, to look at the wounds of the nails in His hands and feet, and to give him something to eat. His followers find it much easier to believe in a ghost than in a flesh-and-blood man brought back to life. After all, they saw Him dead!*

8. *Jesus' resurrection is a down payment and guarantee of every Christian's future resurrection (see 1 Corinthians 15:12–19). Like Him, His people will be raised with physical bodies; we won't float around as disembodied souls. Having a body is part of being fully human. We were created with bodies, and we will have bodies throughout eternity—only they will be perfected, suitable for a life in the presence of God.*

9. *At first the disciples are startled and frightened (see verse 37). They are afraid of ghosts. Then, when they're still struggling to believe their eyes, they have a sense of mingled joy and amazement (see verse 41). Finally, when they are firmly convinced that Jesus is actually alive, they feel great joy and elation (see verse 52).*

10. *Answers will vary. We may believe in the resurrection theoretically, but we need to read and ponder these passages until the words become real for us. We will never have the deep and settled joy of the disciples as long as the resurrection seems like a faraway story.*

11. *The whole story of Jesus—His birth as a human, His life and ministry, His self-offering on the cross, and His resurrection—should move us deeply if it's true (which it is). But His resurrection is the capstone of our joy as Christians because it demonstrates that death—our great enemy—has been defeated. Through Jesus' death on the cross, our sins can be forgiven and we can be truly reconciled with God. Neither we nor anyone else who has faith in Jesus will be destroyed by death.*

12. *Answers will vary.*

13. *Answers will vary.*

14. *Responses will vary.*

Session 3: Joy that Transcends Circumstances

1. *Some of the group members will likely have exciting dreams or a sense of purpose in following Jesus that draws them forward. Others may be worried about aging, loneliness, financial problems, or the illness of a loved one. Make your group a safe place for people to be honest, even if their focus for now is on the negative.*

2. *Answers will vary. Sometimes, people in transition will lose a sense of purpose, either temporarily or permanently. For example, if they are going through life stages such as retirement or having grown children leave the home (empty nest), it can lead to an immediate loss of purpose for them. On the other hand, these life changes can motivate people to refocus their priorities and develop new, long-term plans and goals. Regardless, it's important for each of us to be intentional about seeking God's guidance for the next stage of our lives.*

3. *Some members of your group may be eager to share the challenges they are currently facing, while others may be more reticent. The goal here is for them to share their stories so they can receive encouragement from each other. The group can serve as one of the many ways that God reaches out to them and helps to carry their burdens.*

4. *The simple answer is that it would make a huge difference if we always took our circumstances to Jesus in prayer and then sought to rejoice in Him in spite of what we are facing. This would completely change our outlook and give us the assurance that God is always in control. It would also help us to really notice the blessings that God has provided.*

5. *Negative talk and negative thoughts can drag us down and create a vicious cycle that prevents us from connecting with others and with the joy that Jesus offers. We can become discouraged and lose strength.*

6. *When we feel that we are being dragged down by circumstances, it's important to stop and take a few moments to worship God and express our thankfulness to Him. We can read passages of Scripture that can help us to rejoice. We can also remind ourselves that, if we are followers of Christ, our problems are temporary but God is eternal. In every earthly trial, believers can say, "This too shall pass." There is no need to continue passively obsessing about what is going wrong when we have life in Christ!*

7. *Habakkuk imagines a famine that will come because a foreign army will invade his country, seize Israel's livestock, and destroy their crops. Of course, in such a dire situation—when the people are literally starving—it can be very difficult to remain joyful. This is a situation worse than most of us will ever face, but it shows how we can find joy in any circumstance.*

8. *In order for people to have joy in such a desperate situation, they would have to believe that death by starvation was far from the worst thing that could ever happen to them. They would have to have a hope for the future that wouldn't perish if they themselves physically died. This could take the form of hope for future generations who would survive, or it might take the form of hope in eternal life beyond death for the redeemed of God.*

9. *Habakkuk writes that his "heart pounded" at the thought of an invading army (verse 16). He is clearly feeling terror and dread—and for good reason, as the Babylonians (under their king Nebuchadnezzar II) had a reputation for being brutal in their quest for power.*

10. *Habakkuk recognizes "the Sovereign Lord" is his strength (verse 19), and that God is in control regardless of the circumstances. His total trust in the Lord enables him to reach a place of settled joy. He has confidence that his* *nation isn't going to be completely wiped out because of God's covenant with Abraham. Also, as a man of God, he knows he has a future beyond death.*

11. *Each person's answer will depend on their confidence that they have a future secured beyond their life on this earth—and that regardless of what happens here, they can always look to that greater hope. Of course, this only comes by believing in Christ, trusting Him as Savior, and giving Him the control as Lord.*

12. *Answers will vary.*

13. *Answers will vary.*

14. *Responses will vary.*

Session 4: Joy and Strength

1. *Answers will vary. The point here is for group members to identify some area where the joy of the Lord can be of immediate, practical help to them.*

2. *It's fine if the group members do not report any measurable change at this point—but you can celebrate with those who are aware of a difference!*

3. *Focusing on Christ throughout the day can be as simple as developing the habit of turning our minds to one-sentence prayers each hour. For example, we could say, "Jesus, You are my joy." If we turn our minds to Him as we go through our day, we will end up spending a lot of time praising Jesus and keeping Him at the forefront of our thoughts. We can make this our habit before we check our phones or start worrying about things we can't control. Listening to Christian music or sermon podcasts can also keep our minds on Christ.*

4. *When we're confronted with someone who irritates us, one tactic we can use is to try to see that person from God's perspective. Focusing on Jesus and training our minds to stay aware of Him gives us more grace to deal with* *the difficult people in our lives. Christians can also certainly pray for God's patience and wisdom as we interact with that person!*

5. *We may feel strong because we have a natural take-charge personality or because we had a secure childhood that gave us a stable foundation for life. However, in reality, we are all weak and in need of Jesus' strength—some of us are just more aware of that fact. The irony is that we grow stronger only as we become aware of our need for Jesus' strength and develop a habit of leaning on Him.*

6. *Having joy will help us persevere when things are hard. Knowing that the Lord is completely trustworthy can give His people a reservoir of joy to draw from when life is hard. Likewise, continually rehearsing an attitude of joy can build trust in Him. Just praying, "You are my joy, Jesus," or "I trust You, Jesus," throughout the day can refocus our thoughts on God, help us recognize our blessings, and build our trust in Him.*

7. *In verse 6, we see that before the Word of God was read, the people expressed their respect and reverence for the Lord by worshiping Him. They stood, raised their hands, cried out "Amen," and bowed with their faces to the ground. All of this displayed their devotion to God and their attitude of trusting humility toward Him.*

8. *The people possibly wept because they understood why the Lord had exiled their parents and grandparents from the Promised Land. When they heard the requirements of God's Law, they understood that they and their forebears had fallen terribly short of obeying it. They felt convicted and penitent.*

9. *Nehemiah certainly understood that conviction and repentance are good— without them, none of us would come to authentic faith. However, this was a day for celebrating the fact that God had forgiven His wayward, repentant people and brought them back to their homeland. Also, the people needed to be strong to face the many challenges of rebuilding a nation with hostile neighbors. As Nehemiah said, the true joy that comes from the Lord would be their source of strength.*

10. *Although it is important for followers of Christ to be reverent toward the Lord, the strength we need to live lives of courageous faith comes from the deep joy of knowing we have been forgiven by a God who is not only holy but also loving. Joy in the face of hardship is what carries believers through. The joy of knowing that we are God's children gives us strength.*

11. *In verse 12, we read that the people celebrated with joy simply because they finally understood what God was saying in His Word. This is something we can easily take for granted—but they didn't. We have the incredible privilege of having clear translations of the Bible that are easily accessible, as well as numerous sources of good teaching about God's Word. However, in Nehemiah's day, when books were reproduced with crude writing materials, and most people couldn't read, it was a privilege to hear the Word of God. We need to cultivate that same gratitude when we read the Scriptures and understand what God is asking of us.*

12. *Answers will vary.*

13. *Answers will vary.*

14. *Responses will vary.*

Session 5: Joy Despite Fear

1. *Likely answers include terrorism, car accidents, the loss of jobs, illnesses, poverty, the loss of loved ones—the world is full of things that might happen to us or that are happening to us. God understands that we have to deal with fear.*

2. *Christians are "masters of their souls" in the sense that they are secure in where they are headed when this life on earth is over. As Paul wrote, "We are more than conquerors through him who loved us" (Romans 8:37). Believers in Christ have received the promises of God and are assured that they will be with Him for eternity in spite of the fears they are facing now. Cyprian—who came from a comfortable background as a citizen of the world superpower of* *his day—understood Christians possessed a security in their souls because of Christ's mastery over death and pain and evil.*

3. *Answers will vary. Worry is meditating on fear. It focuses on things that haven't happened yet and may never happen. Fear can be a normal response to a legitimate threat. It can even be a positive force, in that it can motivate us to make sensible precautions (such as preparing for a hurricane or earthquake or quickly exiting the path of danger). Worry goes beyond sensible precautions to paralyzing emotion. It is a habit we are wise to break.*

4. *One way believers in Christ can constructively deal with fear is to remember that God is greater than anything they will ever confront on this earth. Throughout the Bible, God tells His people to not give in to fear (see Joshua 1:9; Psalm 23:4; Isaiah 43:1; Matthew 6:34; John 14:27). It is also important to remember that nothing we fear can ever separate us from God's love (see Romans 8:38–39), so nothing we fear can ultimately harm us in the eternal sense.*

5. *One tactic we can employ to deal with fear of the future is to remind ourselves that God is infinite and we are not (see Revelation 1:8). We don't have to know the answer to every little step along the way to actively follow Him. It's better to ask, "God, what step do You want me to take next?" Instead of obsessing about the path, we start with the present moment and trustfully seek to find God's way forward as we follow Him. We also remember that He is always with His children.*

6. *God rarely answers the question of why He "allowed" something to happen, especially soon after the event. It's unlikely that we would be able to understand the full complexity of the answer even if He did. God's viewpoint and purposes are so much higher than our own (see Isaiah 55:9). The question often has the flavor of accusation, and He would prefer that we trust His character based on what His Word says and the many good things He has done for us (including sending Jesus to die for us) instead of demanding answers about the few confusing things that have taken place.*

7. The appearance of the angel must have been terrifying to the women, because even the tough Roman soldiers were afraid when they saw him (see verse 4). It's interesting to note that the women weren't afraid of the soldiers anymore—they were afraid of the angel and of the strange thing he said to them. The idea of someone rising from the dead wasn't something they could easily wrap their minds around, so they were frightened about this turn of events.

8. The news of the resurrection was so far beyond the women's wildest dreams that they were overflowing with joy even though they were still afraid of the angel and other strange occurrences. The key to their joy was that they had something wonderful to focus on: a living Savior!

9. Answers will vary, but the resurrection of Jesus continues to be extraordinary and wonderful news for followers of Christ— if they don't take it for granted. The resurrection carries with it a promise that we too can be raised from death. Death doesn't have to frighten us anymore. If we can keep our focus on Jesus and His resurrection, we can peacefully withstand scary circumstances.

10. The women got down on their hands and knees in complete humility when they saw that Jesus was alive. This was a posture of worship— worshiping Him for who He is, the Son of God, who had triumphed over death itself! They had to touch Him to be sure He was real and not a ghost or a vision—and the part of Him they touched, His feet, represented the lowest and humblest part. This is a good attitude for us to have toward Jesus.

11. Jesus wasn't scolding the women for a lack of faith or anything of that nature but was simply reassuring them. He understood that fear was natural under those circumstances. God doesn't fault us for being afraid of genuinely frightening situations. He wants to reassure us that we can put aside our fear by focusing on His presence with us.

12. Answers will vary.

13. *Answers will vary.*

14. *Responses will vary.*

Session 6: Joy and Healing

1. *Not everyone in the group will have experienced the need for healing, but it is fairly widespread. Allow the group members to share their experiences, and continue to make your group time a safe place where people can talk about their needs.*

2. *Answers don't need to refer to dramatic or obviously miraculous healings. People can be healed through the use of medication or other treatment, which are also gifts from God. Emotions and relationships can be healed as well, not just our physical bodies.*

3. *Many people try to hide this feeling of weakness and helplessness, but the better response is to take such feelings to God and allow Him to be our strength. As Paul wrote, "That is why, for Christ's sake, I delight in weaknesses, in insults, in hardships, in persecutions, in difficulties. For when I am weak, then I am strong" (2 Corinthians 12:10). It's also good to have one or two trusted people in our lives who get to know us in all our weakness and accept us anyway.*

4. *Answers will vary. One helpful practice is to devote a chunk of time each day—or brief moments frequently throughout each day—to just resting in Jesus' care. This means not worrying or anxiously praying about something, but simply allowing oneself to be in His presence. A person can then take that attitude of rest into a busy day. We can also keep turning our thoughts back to Him, reminding ourselves that His watchful care is constant.*

5. *When it comes to pouring out our hearts to the Lord for healing, awe and respect for God are vital, but so is childlike trust in Him. We need to let down the barriers of embarrassment and mistrust when we go to God with* *our needs, recognizing that He can handle our emotions. We also need to be convinced that He wants to respond to His children with mercy and deep emotional healing—if not with total physical healing right away.*

6. *Emotional wounds are often rooted in feelings such as rejection and abandonment. Being completely understood by someone who is constantly present with us can heal the sensation of being rejected and abandoned. Every child of God is fully accepted by someone who fully knows and fully understands him or her. Nothing is hidden, and yet we are completely loved!*

7. *As we have seen, sometimes God responds quickly to our prayers, while at other times He allows time to pass in order to encourage us to be persistent. Slow healing and partial healing are invitations for us to have greater faith in Him. Christians can continue in joy because we know that God is with us in our illness or woundedness.*

8. *We can still have joy because of who God is and because of all the other good things He has done and continues to do in our lives. It's human nature to focus on the one or two things that may be going wrong while so many other things are good. We need to resist that tendency and consciously choose to pay attention to the good things God has provided.*

9. *The psalmist focuses on what God wants from the relationship rather than solely on his own need. He sees the Lord as desiring to be praised, and he points out that if he's dead in the grave, he won't be able to praise God. This attitude might seem surprising to us, but it is a logical and true concept, and one that turns up several times in the psalms.*

10. *The psalmist speaks about the reversal that took place in his life because of God's mercy. He went from wailing in distress to dancing in celebration. God removed his garments of mourning and clothed him in something for joyful occasions. A robust outward expression of joy comes naturally to him in response. In the same way, at times it can be good for us to let down our inhibitions and really celebrate the good things the Lord has done.*

11. *Answers will vary. It's significant that the psalmist doesn't think of healing as something he deserves. It's an undeserved gift, so he calls it mercy. We have no reason to resent God if He doesn't heal us, because every act of healing is a gesture of undeserved mercy.*

12. *Answers will vary.*

13. *Answers will vary.*

14. *Responses will vary.*

Session 7: Joy in Singing

1. *Answers will vary. Some of us are more gifted musically than others, but even those who don't have a great voice can still express joy to God through singing. The Bible says to "make a joyful noise unto the LORD" (Psalm 100:1 KJV), regardless of what we sound like to others!*

2. *Take a few minutes to discuss some of the songs and hymns that the group members like to sing, and why those songs are especially meaningful to them.*

3. *Singing Jesus' name gives Him honor. It also draws His followers closer to Him and helps them find strength in His Presence. Praising God (in whatever form) drives away spiritual enemies.*

4. *Group members may be struggling to spend daily time in Jesus' presence due to busyness and distraction or a lack of connectedness with Him (treating it as a duty rather than a relationship). Encourage them to treat spending time with God like they would with a friend—not as an obligation but just as the chance to get together. Making the time to spend five minutes with God in the morning or evening is a good place to start. Some things they can do to protect this time is to periodically check in with one another. In the end, they will find that spending time with Jesus will dramatically help their daily lives to be richer and more purposeful.*

5. *Answers will vary. Many churches today are moving away from the more traditional Christmas carols (such as "Hark, the Herald Angels Sing," "The First Noel," or "Joy to the World") in favor of more modern songs. However, regardless of the type of music, we all have songs with lyrics that especially resonate with us. Have some fun with this question and allow the group members a few minutes to discuss their favorite Christmas songs.*

6. *Again, even if we can barely carry a tune, we can still glorify God through song and let the music raise our spirits. We can choose a worship service where we're not just being entertained by the musicians but are also entering into the music in worship.*

7. *David imagined that everything on earth was made by the Lord and so has a way of glorifying the Lord—expressing who He is, putting Him on display, reflecting His creativity and care—that can be likened to singing. Singing is at the essence of praise. The psalms themselves were meant to be sung, not just recited.*

8. *David wanted the earth to sing about the salvation God offers, God's marvelous deeds of creating and rescuing people, His splendor, His majesty, His strength, His joy, His kingship, and finally, the fact that He is coming to restore justice to the earth.*

9. *The psalm celebrates these things by calling attention to the Lord's deeds and attributes. Words such as splendor and majesty urge us to consider the qualities of the Lord that should inspire joy in us. Likewise, the act of singing produces joy. It would be easy to choose favorite lines from the psalm that especially spark joy in us. (Do this as a group if there is time.)*

10. *Whales sing. Waves crash on the shore. Seagulls cry out in flight. The psalmist imagines the sea as full of living creatures whose expression of God's design creates a kind of harmonious music. It is as if ocean creatures have a certain joy in being what they were created to be. We too can enter into that joy by coming into harmony with the way we were created.*

11. *Answers will vary. Hopefully, the group members have become more aware of the central role singing can have in feeding their joy in the Lord.*

12. *Answers will vary.*

13. *Answers will vary.*

14. *Responses will vary.*

Session 8: Joy Even in Suffering

1. *Answers will vary. The group members can get to know some of the deep things that have happened in one another's pasts through this question, so take some time to process their responses. Don't underestimate the gift you can give someone when you truly listen to their story of pain. (Remember to ask the group to limit their stories to two or three minutes per person.)*

2. *As the group leader, you will quickly get a sense of those who were sustained by the Lord during this difficult time and those who toughed it out by sheer willpower. The help of friends and family may have also been vital.*

3. *The first key to a fruitful response when faced with anxiety is to go to God with our worries and pour out our hearts to Him. After this—and this is a second important key—we need to spend time listening to Him while He offers comfort to us. We might spend some time in a Scripture passage that we feel especially speaks to our situation.*

4. *Some people might still be having trouble with experiencing joy even now. Once again, make your group a safe place for them to be honest about their feelings. Hopefully they are now glimpsing what true joy can look like as they spend time with God each day. Celebrate the joy that group members are gaining.*

5. *The main reason that God is a greater source of joy than anything in this world is that He is permanent and everlasting. Death can take away our* *loved ones, and circumstances can take away the things we treasure, but the Lord "is the everlasting God. . . . He will not grow tired or weary, and his understanding no one can fathom" (Isaiah 40:28). Aging, death, and decay are inevitable, so we desperately need to attach our joy to the One who will never fail us or change.*

6. *Answers will vary. Our feelings come and go—and God doesn't always give us a consoling sense of His presence when we are in prayer. Sometimes we need to rely on the promise of His presence—and the promises of His Word— without those good feelings. Feelings have their place, but God doesn't want His children to rely on them for their faith.*

7. *Paul and Silas were stripped of their clothes, which was a humiliating experience, and beaten with rods. They were thrown into a prison with their feet in stocks, which immobilized them and forced them to lie on their backs with no way to roll over or shift position.*

8. *Paul and Silas were in Philippi to take the good news of Jesus to people who knew nothing of Him. Once they were in prison, they chose to take the view that they now had a captive audience (their fellow prisoners) who would learn about Jesus from the way His representatives handled their suffering. Every word they prayed and sang was meant to be heard not only by God but also by their fellow prisoners. As Christians, we often forget that the people around us are watching us every day, and they notice how we act. In addition to their evangelistic aim, Paul and Silas knew that rejoicing in the Lord was the best way for them to deal with suffering. Their pain would be lessened if they focused on the Lord.*

9. *The jailer might have previously heard that Paul cast out the demon from the slave (see verses 16–18). He may have seen Paul and Silas being beaten. He saw them locked up in his prison. He probably heard them singing and praying, so he knew they represented some god or other. Then he felt the earthquake and saw that the prison doors were all open. Knowing that the magistrates would* *likely have him executed if his prisoners escaped, he prepared to kill himself. But then he heard Paul reassure him, and now, in utter fear of Paul's unknown God, he asked what he needed to do to be saved from God's anger. Then he and his household heard a coherent account of Jesus' death, resurrection, and kingship. He cleaned Paul and Silas's wounds and was baptized with his household. What an emotional roller coaster of a night!*

10. *No, Paul and Silas's joy would have been just as valid without a miracle following it. It would still have sent a powerful message to their fellow prisoners and brought glory to God. It would still have been good for Paul and Silas's own souls as well.*

11. *It's important to see in this story that for Paul and Silas, joy was an attitude they chose to have in an excruciating circumstance. They chose to let the wonder of what God had done for them in Christ permeate their reality so that, even after being brutally beaten, they could still sing praise to God. Joy is a choice for each of us as well.*

12. *Answers will vary.*

13. *Answers will vary.*

14. *Responses will vary.*

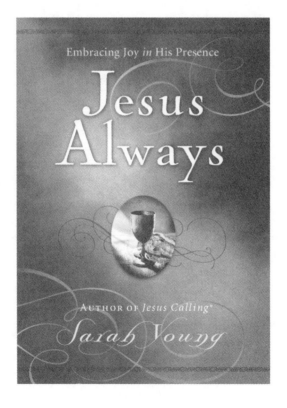

Also available in the
JESUS ALWAYS® BIBLE STUDY SERIES

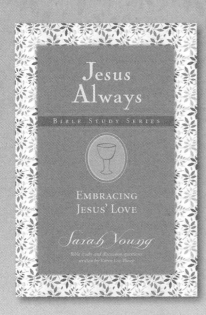

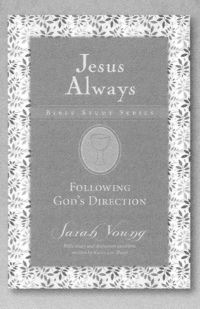

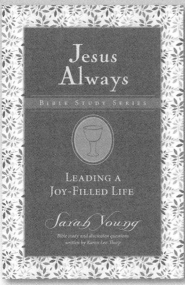

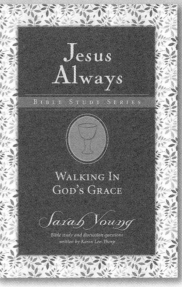

Also Available in the
Jesus Calling® Bible Study Series

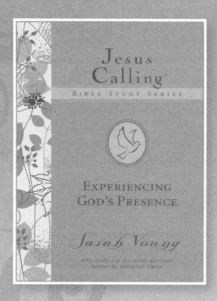

EXPERIENCING GOD'S PRESENCE

Sarah Young

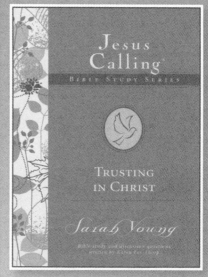

TRUSTING IN CHRIST

Sarah Young

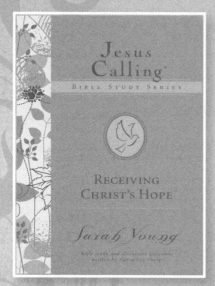

RECEIVING CHRIST'S HOPE

Sarah Young

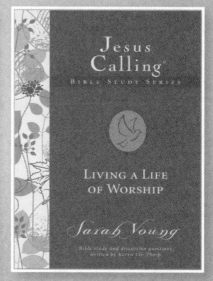

LIVING A LIFE OF WORSHIP

Sarah Young

Also Available in the
Jesus Calling® Bible Study Series

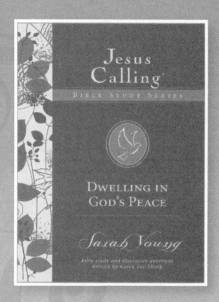

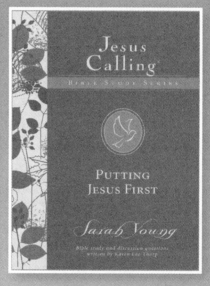

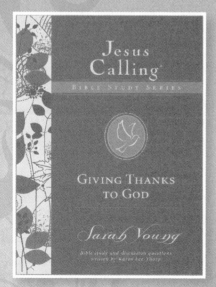

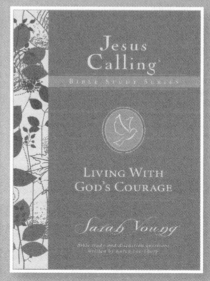

If you liked reading this book, you may enjoy these other titles by *Sarah Young*

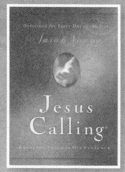

Jesus Calling®
Hardcover

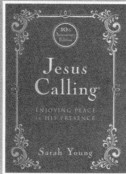

Jesus Calling® 10th Anniversary Edition
Bonded Leather

Peace in His Presence:
Favorite Quotations from Jesus Calling®
Padded Hardcover

Jesus Calling® for Kids
Hardcover

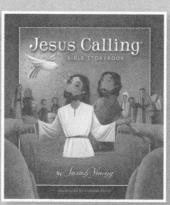

Jesus Calling® Bible Storybook
Hardcover

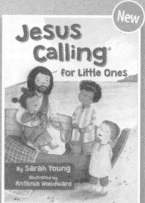

Jesus Calling® for Little Ones
Board Book